All Dolls are Collectible

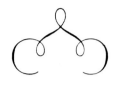

All Dolls are Collectible

by Genevieve Angione
and Judith Whorton

CROWN PUBLISHERS, INC., NEW YORK

Prepared and published by Everybodys Press, Inc., Hanover, Pennsylvania 17331
Printed in the United States of America

This edition prepared for distribution by
CROWN PUBLISHERS, INC.

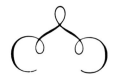

Acknowledgments

The dolls illustrated in this book have come from various collections. The authors wish to thank these collectors and museums for their kind cooperation and assistance. Their dolls represented in the illustrations, are listed here by illustration number and collector's name.

1–Angione Collection
2–Angione Collection
3–Whorton Collection
4–Angione Collection
5A–Whorton Collection
5B–Angione Collection
5C–Angione Collection
6A–Angione Collection
6B–Angione Collection
7–Angione Collection
8–Angione Collection
9A–Angione Collection
9B–Angione Collection
10–Angione Collection
11–Angione Collection
12A–Angione Collection
12B–Angione Collection
13–Angione Collection
14A–Strong Collection
14B–Strong Collection
15–Skuet Collection
16–Sims Collection
17–Angione Collection
18–Angione Collection
19–Angione Collection
20–Smith Collection
21–Sims Collection
22–Whorton Collection
23–Angione Collection
24–Angione Collection
25–Angione Collection
26–Angione Collection
27–Sims Collection

28–Sims Collection
29–Sims Collection
30–Callaway Collection
31–Whorton Collection
32–Angione Collection
33–Angione Collection
34–Sims Collection
35A–Angione Collection
35B–Angione Collection
36–Angione Collection
37–Briley Collection
38–Brett Collection
39–Davies Collection
40A–Briley Collection
40B–Briley Collection
41–Whorton Collection
42–Angione Collection
43–Angione Collection
44–Angione Collection
45A–Sims Collection
45B–Sims Collection
45C–Sims Collection
46A–Angione Collection
46B–Angione Collection
47A–Whorton Collection
47B–Whorton Collection
47C–Whorton Collection
47D–Whorton Collection
48–Angione Collection
49–Strong Collection
50A–Angione Collection
50B–Angione Collection
51–Angione Collection

52–Angione Collection
53–Angione Collection
54–Whorton Collection
55–Angione Collection
56–Angione Collection
57A–Angione Collection
57B–Angione Collection
58–Whorton Collection
59A–Whorton Collection
59B–Whorton Collection
59C–Burr Collection
60–Whorton Collection
61–Angione Collection
62A–Angione Collection
62B–Angione Collection
63A–Sims Collection
63B–Sims Collection
64–Angione Collection
65–Whorton Collection
66–Whorton Collection
67–Angione Collection
68–Whorton Collection
69–Angione Collection
70–Sims Collection
71–Sims Collection
72–Angione Collection
73–Angione Collection
74–Whorton Collection
75–Angione Collection
76A–Spinning Wheel's
  Complete Book of Dolls
76B–Spinning Wheel's
  Complete Book of Dolls

188A–Angione Collection
188B–Angione Collection
189–Whorton Collection
190A–Angione Collection
190B–Angione Collection
191A–Angione Collection
191B–Angione Collection
192A–Angione Collection
192B–Angione Collection
193A–Angione Collection
193B–Angione Collection
194A–Angione Collection
194B–Angione Collection
195A–Angione Collection
195B–Angione Collection
196A–Angione Collection
196B–Angione Collection
197A–Angione Collection
197B–Angione Collection
198–Angione Collection
199A–Strong Collection
199B–Strong Collection
200–Angione Collection
201A–Angione Collection
201B–Angione Collection
201C–Angione Collection
202–Whorton Collection
203–Whorton Collection
204–Angione Collection
205–Angione Collection
206–Angione Collection
207–Angione Collection
208–Angione Collection
209–Angione Collection
210A–Sims Collection
210B–Sims Collection
211–Angione Collection
212–Whorton Collection
213–Whorton Collection
214–Angione Collection
215–Brett Collection
216–Huff Collection
217A–Whorton Collection
217B–Whorton Collection
218A–Angione Collection
218B–Sims Collection
219–Whorton Collection

220–Wynn Collection
221–Whorton Collection
222–Callaway Collection
223A–Angione Collection
223B–Angione Collection
224A–Angione Collection
224B–Angione Collection
225A–Angione Collection
225B–Angione Collection
226A–Angione Collection
226B–Angione Collection
227–Angione Collection
228–Angione Collection
229–Callaway Collection
230A–Whorton Collection
230B–Whorton Collection
231–Whorton Collection
232–Briley Collection
233–Sims Collection
234–Whorton Collection
235–Whorton Collection
236–Angione Collection
237A–Angione Collection
237B–Angione Collection
238–Huff Collection
239–Huff Collection
240–Strong Collection
241–Angione Collection
242A–Angione Collection
242B–Angione Collection
243–Callaway Collection
244–Callaway Collection
245–Callaway Collection
246–Callaway Collection
247–Callaway Collection
248–Angione Collection
249–Angione Collection
250A–Angione Collection
250B–Angione Collection
251A–Angione Collection
251B–Angione Collection
252–Angione Collection
253–Whorton Collection
254A–Angione Collection
254B–Angione Collection
255A–Angione Collection
255B–Angione Collection

256–Angione Collection
257–Whorton Collection
258A–Brewer Collection
258B–Brewer Collection
259A–Angione Collection
259B–Angione Collection
260–Angione Collection
261–Angione Collection
262A–Angione Collection
262B–Angione Collection
263A–Angione Collection
263B–Angione Collection
264–Angione Collection
265A–Angione Collection
265B–Angione Collection
266–Whorton Collection
267–Whorton Collection
268A–Angione Collection
268B–Angione Collection
269–Angione Collection
270–Sims Collection
271–Sims Collection
272–Whorton Collection
273–Whorton Collection
274–Whorton Collection
275A–Angione Collection
275B–Angione Collection
276A–Angione Collection
276B–Angione Collection
277–Whorton Collection
278–Angione Collection
279–Angione Collection
280–Whorton Collection
281–Whorton Collection
282A–Whorton Collection
282B–Whorton Collection
283A–Angione Collection
283B–Angione Collection
284–Angione Collection
285A–Angione Collection
285B–Angione Collection
286–Angione Collection
287–Whorton Collection
288–Whorton Collection
289A–Angione Collection
289B–Angione Collection
290A–Angione Collection

Photographers:

Joe Aloia, III
Ralph Anderson
Charles Angione
R. Bryan Sims
J. Roddy Sims

Contents

To my dear friend
Margaret Woodbury Strong
March 20, 1897–July 17, 1969
with fond memories

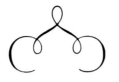

Notes from the Authors

This is not a pretty picture book about dolls for those who like to look and run. It is not a price book, nor a parade of a collection, nor a dictionary to compete with the excellent ones already available. Rather it is a textbook on how to collect dolls. It is designed for both the novice, eager to invest in a new hobby about which she knows almost nothing, and for the established collector who searches for special dolls, undeterred by their scarcity.

Doll collecting, except perhaps for gift dolls, has never been an inexpensive hobby, and it behooves every collector to know what to look for when buying and how best to safeguard monetary investments. Zest for the hunt, enthralling as it may be, should be tempered with knowledge, and knowledge can only be acquired through diligent study or by sad experience; the latter can be costly.

In my twenty-three years of collecting, buying, selling, studying, and writing about dolls, thousands of letters have crossed my desk; most of them contained questions. Always the same subjects kept cropping up—every week of every year, from every direction.

Since one typewriter cannot supply all the answers individually no matter how much effort is expended on the attempt, a book, combining the repeated questions and answers, seems a logical solution, even though a book is not the easiest project in the world, and an instruction book is more difficult than most.

This book is dedicated to my good friend, Margaret Strong, whose legacy to doll collectors is contained in The Margaret Woodbury Strong Museum, located on her estate in this city of Rochester, New York. The 30,000 dolls it houses are of all types. Because she was a tremendously wealthy woman, one would suppose that only the world's rarest dolls would grace such a collection, but not so.

"Little girls did not look at the marks on the backs of doll heads," she protested when anyone criticized the addition of very ordinary dolls. "There were dolls under every Christmas tree in America and little girls loved all of them. Just look at the condition some of the poor things are in now from too much loving."

We discussed dolls endlessly for years, early in the day and far into many nights, often with great disagreement, but our interest in dolls was omniverous.

Although she did not live to see the publication of *All-Bisque and Half-*

Bisque Dolls, released less than a month after her death, she enjoyed supplying rare dolls from her collection for that volume and followed the accumulation of the material with lively interest.

"But all dolls are collectible," she insisted. "Why don't you write another book and prove it?" We were planning to do just that.

So, for you, and for Margaret, this book has been written.

Genevieve Angione
Rochester, N.Y.

A Note From Judith Whorton

Genevieve and I were sitting at her round kitchen table when I became involved with Book II (All Dolls are Collectible). We were enjoying a late night snack. My visiting family and Genevieve's daughter had been asleep for hours.

Instead of talking about dolls our conversation turned to books. Genevieve named an author whose study of patents had set standards for research. "But a lot of the information doesn't help a collector decide if a doll is common or rare. There's not even a book with a clear definition of paperweight eyes," I said.

Genevieve began to ask my opinion of numerous books. I felt as if I were having an oral examination. Without comment, my hostess suddenly rose from the table and walked out of the room. What did I say wrong, I wondered.

In moments Genevieve came out of her office and placed a bound manuscript in front of me.

"You are the first person to see this. Not even my family has read my new book."

As I read the pages, a transformation happened. I forgot that my friend had a collection before I was old enough to say the word "doll." Enthusiastically I began to give comments. It was thrilling to find a book with so much information.

Before refiling the manuscript Genevieve showed me the way she put a book together. I listened politely but I couldn't imagine how this would be used by me.

When I returned home our letters often included a discussion of Book II. "When are you going to study writing?" Genevieve asked. Occasionally she would send me a doll book with the challenge "Find the errors."

The summer after Genevieve died I visited Rochester, determined to talk her family into finishing her work. "No," replied her daughter, "we have decided you should do it."

Genevieve had made meticulous notes listing the dolls which should be included. When she bought a doll it was photographed and a description in her fresh style was indexed. Other information has been taken from her generous letters to her hundreds of collector friends. The inclusion of a plastic limited edition doll is one of the few additions to Genevieve's ideas. But as she was always interested in new concepts, surely this would have been included.

Genevieve was an unusual person who cared about everything that happened around her. She was willing to go out into a rainstorm to prop up a nest to protect three baby redbirds. Yet when reviewing a doll book she never hesitated to say if it was filled with errors.

She believed the best way to enjoy a hobby is to study it with a realistic attitude. So for you, Genevieve, who taught so many, this book has been completed.

—Judith Whorton
Birmingham, Alabama

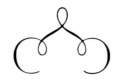

Introduction to Doll Collecting

If you want to invite friends for dinner, but have never so much as boiled a potato, you are going to have to acquire a cookbook somewhere. So let this be your Collecting Cookbook. First let's talk about collecting in general before we talk about dolls in particular, for the same generalizations apply.

The biggest handicap to collecting anything is in the initial enthusiasm. The average novice jumps gleefully overboard and wishes too late he'd learned to swim; he may be years selling his original errors.

Why is it that some people have immense fun collecting and every one of their investments seems to prove profitable, while others, just as willing, are forever running into heartaches, even financial loss? Luck is not the answer, for luck is not consistent. The answer lies in preparation—the willingness to study, to observe, to know before the buying starts, and above all, in the self-discipline to say "No," frequently and firmly, to super-salesmen and to oneself and "Yes," when a good piece is offered.

The fun of collecting comes from knowing what you are doing and being able to do it at the most propitious moment. If you study in the field you have chosen, if you never miss an opportunity to visit established collections, if you ask questions and check the answers until you never have to ask these same questions again, you are becoming a collector instead of a gatherer.

If you make up your mind about what you want to collect, if you accept the fact that you may never find some of the things on your list, yet never give up hope of finding them, if your enthusiasm does not wane through endless look-ing, then you are learning to enjoy whatever hobby enticed you in the first place.

Almost everyone gets a tremendous bargain once in a lifetime. Such windfalls come about when the seller does not take time to identify his merchandise properly, but the buyer recognizes exactly what it is. The world is full of what collectors call "sleepers"—items which have a value unknown to the seller or owner. Only if you know your own field inside and out can you expect to find sleepers. Obviously no one can point them out to you.

If you find a sleeper at a dealer's shop or antiques show counter, you are under no obligation to do anything but purchase; it is not necessary to point out to the seller the error of his ways, any more than you should expect him to confide that his merchandise is overpriced or not what it appears to be. Your good buy is your reward for studying.

However, if you find a sleeper in a home, many of us believe you should not take advantage of the nice person who has saved the treasures through the years for you to find.

You will undoubtedly hear that if you offer a fair price, the owner will think the item is far more valuable than it is and refuse to sell it. In twenty-three years of buying and selling, this writer has found just the opposite to be true. Recently, on two social calls, three beautiful sleepers were found being used just as ornaments in homes. In each instance the owner said, "Oh, everyone wants that." Without any sales pressure at all, an honorable price in today's market was offered for each item. The owners were amazed. Within two days, all three pieces were brought to the door. Apparently the "everybody" who had wanted them had underestimated the common sense of the owners.

On the other hand, if someone demands a price beyond the worth of the piece, refuse to buy it, no matter how badly you want it. An even better one may be waiting you around the corner. Except for handmade articles, few items ever went into the market as one-of-a-kind. Manufacturers of almost everything had to sell in quantity to stay in business. You can be sure that items were made in great quantities, widely distributed, and are still waiting somewhere for you to find.

This mass production is the best reason for dropping the word "rare" from collectors' and dealers' vocabularies. "Uncommon" is one thing, and often quite true; "rare", in many instances, is a gross exaggeration. Truly rare articles are not offered to casual shoppers, nor would they remain to gather dust on dealers' shelves.

Where does a collector get information? Anywhere and everywhere. Collecting is not an exact science by any means and it is only in the past three decades that a serious effort has been made, especially in the doll field, to assemble the information which is now available.

Facts do not change, but methods of comparison change; new material is uncovered; overwhelming evidence piles up to undermine what was thought to be a fact. Collectors should watch this progress and know all the newest data. The only place such information is available is in books and specialized magazines.

Complaints are rife that various authors do not agree on this or that point, that one book or another is in error, or that collectors have to buy too many books to get the whole story. All these problems are present in most collecting fields.

Yet few books are published that have no value. Perhaps just the pictures are worth the price. Every book elaborates on something of interest to the author. Even if some of the elaboration is wrong, collectors are forever meeting people who have never gone past the incorrect state; it is the collector who must know better.

The early doll books were friendly cooperative affairs with much of the information contributed by the hobbyists themselves. It is doubtful that the authors, personally well-loved by the collectors of their day, had any idea they were opening up a whole new area of serious research. Too

often they relied on an owner's enthusiastic appraisal of her collection, and too often people will imbue their possessions with qualities they do not possess.

Today some researchers travel all over the world seeking more information. Others stay at home and buy dolls of the widest possible variety and learn what those dolls can tell them. Both systems work well and complement each other. The traveler finds references to many dolls; quite often the homebound creature finds one to examine.

So spend your first money on books, and spend your first time finding out what is in them. Borrow the books if you can and make sure which you want for your guides before you purchase them. Get sample copies of specialized magazines or borrow them from your public library until you decide which ones best suit your needs. Back issues will do nicely.

Through the printed word and illustrations, you learn the necessary vocabulary of collecting. Until you have seen good pictures or detailed drawings of patterns, trims shapes, and comparative sizes, identifying words will have no exact meaning for you. When you have seen and possibly handled rare or very good items, you will know what to look for when something for sale appeals to you.

Unlike books, magazines will give you the first inkling of present prices. An advertised price is an "asking price" and though it may astonish you, it gives you something with which to compare prices in your own buying area. Many dealers advertise in hope of finding new customers in areas which traditionally have higher prices than local people are willing to pay. Dealers right in your home town may have the same item much cheaper. You will never know what is reasonable if you do not know what you think is unreasonable!

If you are diligent, dolls will come to your attention in many places because you are looking for them, and you will find that a head full of information can be more useful and valuable than a bank full of money. The most desirable and rarest items are seldom offered for public sale except at world famous auction houses, but there is no shortage of ordinary or spurious pieces of anything in any field. The very fact that the money may not be available to make a purchase is often the greatest stroke of luck a collector can have. The satisfaction that accompanies a good purchase is only exceeded by the unhappiness over a bad one.

Keeping Records

Often you will find articles in magazines which you will want to keep for reference, but a helter-skelter clutter of magazines and clippings is no help when you want an answer in a hurry. Serious collectors work out some sort of systematic filing. Here is one that has worked well, is inexpensive, and is not unduly burdensome. Indeed, the burden can be a double pleasure; when you're setting the material up to file—and when you need to find your reference quickly.

On each magazine you buy, mark on the front cover the page numbers that interest you. If you have room, store the whole magazine, filed by years. If not, at the end of the year, cut out the pages you have marked on the cover and put them in ring binders.

Do not glue them to "scrapbook" sheets; years from now the most interesting thing about them may be the advertisements on the reverse side. Instead, buy yourself a 3-hole punch and a roll of inch-wide brown gummed tape. Cut lengths of tape slightly longer than the pages, fold them in half lengthwise, moisten and fasten one to each page you want to save. Trim the ends, and put them through the punch two or three at a time, then fit them into ring binders of the proper size for each magazine you clip. Mark the name of the magazine and the years covered on the spine of the binder.

Reverse filing is convenient for reference purposes. That is, file forward from the back of the book, January to December, thus putting the latest articles in the latest book.

Such scrapbooks have a monetary value in later years far exceeding the subscription costs of the magazines. To make these clippings priceless to you and to the person who eventually buys them, index the material in a bound alphabetized book. It is simple to do, puts the information at your fingertips when you want it.

An index page might look like this:

A

All-bisque	article w/illus	Name of magazine Oct '67
All-bisque	lg. ad w/prices	Name of magazine Dec '68
A.M.	article w/illus	Name of magazine Jan '69
"Alice" bands	article w/variations	Name of magazine Feb '69
A.T.	article w/illus	Name of magazine May '69
A.M. twirler	article w/illus	Name of magazine June '69
Averill, G.	article w/biog	Name of magazine Sept '69
All-bisque	Processes article	Name of magazine Nov '69

The beginning collector in any field must study, examine, ask questions, acquire a pertinent library, and watch the professionals. After that it is safe to proceed with animated caution. Like rearing children, a hobby is supposed to be, and truly can be, interesting and exciting, but it is also time-consuming and a gamble. Successful gamblers are always well informed, alert to the immediate possibilities and, above all, acutely aware of what they are doing.

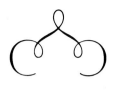

Answers to Questions Commonly Asked

What is a doll?

A doll is a humanized toy, a plaything. Dolls can be of almost any material, produced in a factory, a home, or a studio; they may be old or new, fabulous in detail or plain as dry toast, but they must have play possibilities for a child. A doll must NOT have a base permanently attached or molded to it. Mechanical dolls which are generally attached to music boxes so that they may function properly are still dolls, made for the entertainment of children.

Extraneous material is often included in doll collections. Kate Greenaway and Kewpie salt shakers, figurines holding dolls, creche figures (which are actually religious items), piano babies, swing figures from the bottoms of pulldown lamps are not dolls, even though they are doll oriented. Nor are porcelain pincushions and telephone tops, sometimes referred to as halfdolls; these were created for boudoir and bedroom decorations, not for child play. A doll must have the primary intention of being a toy, even though contemporary artists' dolls may seem too expensive for child's play.

Why collect dolls?

There are as many reasons as there are doll collectors. Some are superficial, like collecting as a status thing, or trying to outdo one's "friend." Some collectors seek to fill a subconscious need—to replace their children who have grown and left the nest or the children they have never had. Others have an overwhelming compassion for damaged or neglected dolls; they buy them, repair them, dress them daintily, then sell them for money to buy more "orphans." Some are motivated by intellectual interest; they buy dolls

to study or write about or keep records for someone else to write about. But most collectors buy dolls simply because they love them—and that is really the best and most satisfactory reason of all.

How expensive is doll collecting?

It's just as expensive as you care to make it. If you want to collect nothing but rare, perfect, and completely dressed dolls, or to assemble a collection overnight, it will mean an outlay of a great deal of money. Fine dolls of any kind command good prices. Many of them are minor works of art just as truly as other small art objects from the same periods. The dictionary defines a hobby as "a thing a person likes to do in his spare time." No matter how you're tempted, the money for the car insurance, the mortgage, or straightening the children's teeth should not be invaded. Children, house, and car are not spare time activities.

If you know you cannot invest several hundred dollars, then set your sights a little lower. You can save up to buy one lovely example and cherish it contentedly. But if the Jumeaux, in this collector's opinion some of the most beautiful dolls the world has ever known, or the old fine German closed-mouth varieties are out of your price reach, consider the open-mouth German dolls which have enchanted little girls in the early part of this century. The varieties of dolls are beyond belief. There is something for everyone.

Is an "inexpensive" collection worthwhile?

Whatever you enjoy to collect and can afford is worthwhile. Often small unpretentious collections have an outstanding characteristic not always found in more elaborate ones—they are precious to their owners and reflect love and attention. Sometimes these dolls are an integral part of the house decor, arranged around old children's nursery furniture. Sometimes they are exhibited in small scenes in shadow boxes or old wall clock cases with carefully selected pieces of dollhouse furniture, or they may fill an ordinary china closet. Many types of dolls can be used in this happy and thoroughly satisfying manner.

After I've studied the books, what next?

If you're smart, you'll start close to home to look in junk stores, house, garage, and church sales, antiques shops and shows, and inquire about dolls among your family and friends. Examine every doll you find and learn to remember what you see. Make notes about the markings if any, the condition and price if the doll is for sale, and file your notes for future reference. Pay special attention to the decorating, that is, the complexion coating, the painted eyes, eyebrows and eyelashes, the cheek coloring, and painting of the hair if it is molded.

Study the eyes and learn to know the difference between French ovals and German rounds, which eyes properly should be set and which eyes should sleep. Examine the type and kind of wig. Inspect the body. Are all the parts there or are some missing? Are some parts replacements? Does the head properly fit the body?

Handle the dolls you examine with respect—no yanking up wigs to look for marks, no undressing dolls without permission, no leaving them undressed if permission is given. Or maybe you'll be satisfied to let the owner handle while you look. Learn what you can from other collectors and interested dealers about their prizes and mistakes. They are wonderful sources of information. However, don't expect even your best friend to take you along when she combs her favorite spots. It's up to you to find your own secret contacts. When you have correlated in your mind what you have learned from your books with what you have observed and have begun to know what to look for, you are ready to begin your buying.

Should I join a club?

That depends on the club. You can usually get yourself invited as a guest to a meeting or two and make up your own mind. If you learn more about the speaker's last trip to Europe than about dolls, if swap and sell meetings predominate, if elaborate lunches or teas make it more of a social affair than a study group, and none of these appeal to you, you may decide to continue as a loner.

Do dolls by modern doll artists belong in my collection?

Original creations by doll artists deserve a place in any comprehensive collection. Plaster of Paris molds can only be used fifty times or less, and often a collector finds, a few years after her purchase, that she has a rare and unusual doll, because the artist has destroyed the molds or taken them out of production for some reason or another.

How about modern reproductions?

Some modern dollmakers specialize only in reproductions of old dolls. Because modern porcelain slip is manufactured under chemical supervision, with the latest mixing and testing equipment, the basic material in many reproductions surpassed the old type in quality. There is no reason in the world why these good reproductions should not be assembled in collections. The big drawback is that generally they must be ordered, with a deposit, then waited for patiently, perhaps several months, because the artists are overloaded with orders. However, many collectors frankly admit that if they were starting in today's high market, they would collect good reproductions.

While excellent modern originals can stand proudly with any group of antique dolls, good reproductions are better confined in one collection by themselves than sprinkled through a collection of old dolls.

How can I tell a modern reproduction?

Some modern reproductions are fantastically good, and if they are not marked it takes an expert to spot them. The superior quality of the material may be the first clue. However, many are marked with the maker's name and year of production, though the markings may be shallow or so small they can only be seen in excellent light.

Once in a while a doll comes to light which has a modern reproduction head on an old original body. On jointed bodies, these are not difficult to identify unless they are unmarked or the mark is at the base of the neck. Incidents where the maker's mark has been removed seldom fool anyone. However, the narrow rim of body kid which overlaps a shoulder plate and has to be glued down to prevent the head from falling off can hide a multitude of sins. Usually the first inkling comes with the price; beginners should be wary about unusually low prices for normally expensive dolls. Seeing and studying all kinds of dolls over and over will lead you to know good quality from bad, excellent workmanship from fair or poor, put-togethers from originals, and old dolls from excellent reproductions.

Many faintly marked and unmarked reproductions have been sold over the years to general dealers who cannot be expected to keep abreast of all the doll reproductions entering the market. Most often these dolls have been included in sale lots; unfortunately they can represent an overall loss to the purchaser. But all good collectors have one trait in common: they cannot be sold something they do not want even if the salesman has the tongue of an angel and the persistence of the F.B.I. When in doubt, don't.

I have a nice collection of dolls, and would like to start a museum. What advice?

Making a collection and remodeling a building to put it in is only the first step. The operation has to be accepted by local civic and zoning authorities, and then by the association of museums. Local requirements about fire and health hazards, liability insurance, and parking areas must be observed. Museum requirements about hours, guides, records, storage, display arrangements, personnel, and management are difficult to meet without unlimited funds.

Then, too, is the matter of patronage. The public is accustomed to museums without admission charges, and very fine museums at that, with constantly changing displays, additional gifts and acquisitions, and often priceless loan material. Think seriously about bucking that system before your plans are too advanced.

Would it help me to sell my unwanted dolls and also to get a discount on dolls I did want if I became a dealer?

Those are advantages, true, but there are other elements involved—government preliminaries before you start and follow-up afterward, and the doll world has a few standards of its own which may give you trouble.

You will need a state or local license to collect taxes on your retail sales, and established dealers will require such a license number along with a signed exemption sheet to justify untaxed sales to you. Records must be kept and periodic reports of your gross and taxable sales must be made, along with prompt payments of taxes collected. Some states also require an annual inventory tax—often you must pay this inventory tax on the same dolls year after year if you do not sell them immediately. There are fines if you do not comply with regulations and, under some unhappy circumstances, your merchandise can be seized.

If I do decide to become a dealer, what are the pros and cons of taking my merchandise to an antiques show or sale?

Crossing a state line to take part in any kind of antiques show or sale makes you subject to the tax rules of that state. Your most important credential will be your dealer tax collection certificate. If you are to avoid paying your sales taxes outside your own area in addition to the local tax collection unit, you must have numbered receipts for taxes paid.

If you go ahead anyway, it will be easier to account for all your doll business if you set up a separate checking account for that money and keep it entirely away from your family finances. Remember the Federal Income tax.

Doll conventions and most antiques shows have limited space and long waiting lists. Many shows now require that all merchandise be marked with accurate information and prices. Dealers have always known they are their own best customers and a surprising amount of buying goes on before the public is admitted. You cannot very well refuse to sell to other dealers, nor can you overprice your things to keep dealers away without keeping the public away as well. Established dealers always have customers quite willing to buy from them but not so willing to buy from strangers, so you may find yourself in the wholesale business or not in business at all.

There are additional problems—the matter of checks. It is the exceptional customer who pays in cash in these days when pickpockets and petty thieves follow shows of all kinds. Some checks are good; some are almost always bad. Through the years and through exchange of information with other dealers, one learns when not to surrender valuable merchandise if it is to be paid for by check.

There is the matter of stealing. You must memorize your inventory, your display, and your sales, and you must know how to protect the things on display. It is a blessing if you have adequate, experienced and honest help. If you are alone, you will have to depend on help from other dealers and it will be a long time before you will feel free to ask for such help or have it offered. It will also be a long time before you know what "floaters" on the floor can be trusted or have trustworthy ones suggested to you. Floaters are visiting dealers without booths, or sometimes experienced collectors who have been pinch-hitting for many years. A show of any kind is a small community where everything eventually happens, including death.

Floaters may guard a booth if a dealer becomes ill, or is called from the floor for long-distance messages, or does not arrive before the show opens. A reliable floater is often the only chance a dealer has to leave the floor for such a simple thing as a hot meal.

Most shows have guards on duty, not only during the night but during visiting hours. Exhibition halls have been known to burn out, and there have been instances where, without night guards, entire accumulations of exhibits in buildings have been removed by professional thieves. Insurance is your responsibility and you will find the rates very high, indeed.

It is almost impossible, too, to protect a loaded station wagon in transit if you are alone. Through the years, even dealers who were not alone have been robbed of their entire stocks at restaurant and motel parking lots, as well as in parking garages. Alarm devices on cars are expensive and sometimes illegal. The insurance companies know all these things and set their rates accordingly.

There are many serious aspects beneath the glamour of a spectacular show. Remember some of them the next time you feel you have been given a short answer by an exhibitor.

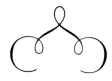

Do's and Don'ts of
Doll Collecting

First and foremost: DON'T take up doll collecting if you hate to make decisions. From the day you buy your first doll until the day you sell the last one, your life will be an endless series of decisions.

In fact, even before you buy your first doll you should decide (1) what your specialty is going to be and, (2) how big your largest doll can be. Just knowing what you want to accomplish will help you put some restraint on your buying, and you will be less tempted by dolls which are merely "cute," or cheap, or "wistful looking."

Unlike many collectibles, dolls require space. If there is a spare room available to you, size need not be a hindrance for your small dolls can then be dolls for big dolls. You are fortunate if you have money and space for glassed cabinets—open shelves are disasterous to most dolls and to all doll clothing. Ordinary mortals, however, have to sandwich their dolls in among other cherished family possessions. Controlling the size of your purchases from the beginning will simplify your display problems as well as your finances.

DON'T start to collect with the thought in your head, "I can always sell them." While it is true someone will have sold the dolls to you, it likely will have been an experienced salesperson in a highly competitive atmosphere of an auction, an antiques show, or a busy shop. You probably paid the "long price," and unless you guess wisely about the trends in buying, you may have to hold them a long time to recover your investment. Haste makes waste of hobby funds, and the collector is responsible for the dolls she buys—don't blame the seller.

So, buy a doll because you like it and are willing to be stuck with it for the rest of your life.

Some of your choices will have no appeal to anyone but yourself; others will attract everyone's attention. Visitors will pester you to sell some dolls; others you might not be able to give away. This means you should buy personally—and for keeps. Even though you do sell some of your dolls later, you should not buy them with selling in mind.

Buying

DON'T confide to everyone you meet that you are "starting a doll collection but don't know much about them." With this approach you are making yourself the target for spellbinders—and some of them are professionals. The proper response when you are asked if you are a doll collector is, "In a small way," and let it go at that. There is always someone around quick to take advantage of your uncertainties. It is not necessary to be their victim.

DON'T buy anyone's "grandmother's doll" until you know what you are doing. Many a grandmother had a doll or two "among her things," but they were not necessarily her childhood dolls. Thousands of grandmothers never had anything but a rag doll or a hand-me-down. Because they never got over the desire for a "real" doll, they managed to acquire one in their later years. Dolls are especially vulnerable to sentimental, exaggerated stories about their age, their past history, and their rarity. It is your responsiblity as a collector to know the difference between fact and fancy.

DON'T believe people who tell you they are showing you a doll even though they have another customer who is dying to have it. If it is worth dying over, the willing one would pay far more than you are asked to pay and without any sales pitch at all. So discount such "favors."

If you are told, "That's exactly the way I found it," you are being warned, at the very least, of irresponsible merchandising. Dolls are hardly passed innocently along from attics to dealers to collectors without arousing any interest somewhere along the line. It would be a miracle if a Bru or an A.T. could be picked up by a collector under such fortuitous negligence. Anyone, be he wholesaler, dealer, or collector who buys dolls without inspecting them is piling up costly trouble.

DON'T buy a collection of parts. Doll hospital owners may be able to use many bits and pieces in time, but the average collector is much wiser to let the doll hospital match the parts you need. Even with 30,000 parts on hand, a parts dealer often cannot find exactly what the customer needs.

DON'T believe wild and wonderful tales. An Armand Marseille is *not* a "French doll made in Germany." (It is a completely German doll and a fairly late one by advanced collector's standards.) The Germans did not make dolls "copying crippled or mentally ill children of their rulers." Most German dolls were modeled by highly competent sculptors; many were patented; and all were made by the thousands, the majority for export. Porcelain manufacturing was an expensive operation and the very idea that the giants in the field would bootleg disparaging portrait dolls is ridiculous. Such stories persist, in print and gossip, simply because some people demand a doll with a "story", even if the story has not a shred of truth.

Buying By Mail

Don't write letters advertising your ignorance. Ask politely for the information you want and omit, "They must be reasonably priced." Prices will not be tailored to the wishes of a stranger. You should include a stamp, rather than a stamped addressed envelope for a reply; generally your envelopes are not the proper size for the information a conscientious dealer is willing to send you, such as lists.

Study and compare the answers you get, then file them for reference. Do not be alarmed when some of your stamps do not come back

home. Many dealers are busier than you think, older than you might believe, and beset with the same woes that keep you from writing home or cleaning behind the piano as often as you should.

In doll collecting, the manufacturers' names are important. They represent the only way one can buy dolls which cannot be examined personally, and the only way dolls can be catalogued in books or for your own records. The modern collector who, through advertising or correspondence, is seriously searching for an **S & H 948 15** is using the manufacturer's name, the stock number, and the size figure to identify the doll she wants. To this she can add her own preference for brown eyes "if possible," a human hair wig, dressed or undressed, mint or average condition.

Because dolls were produced in such hundreds of thousands, the manufacturers made it easier for themselves, their employees, and their customers by using incised marks as part of the casting molds. It was in a way a subtle form of advertising. It is also a boon to today's collector—something the manufacturer probably never thought of.

DON'T send money off to the four winds without checking the reputation of the dealer. Just because someone pays for an advertisement is no proof he has a reputation like Macy's or Bailey, Banks & Biddle.

An advertiser may be merely a go-between, a person who learns what dolls a collector wants to dispose of, agrees on a price with the owner, proceeds to advertise them, and sells them at an advantageous mark-up to himself. Should you wish to return such a purchase, chances are poor. The original owner will be in no haste to refund your money to the go-between and take back an unwanted article.

If you are satisfied you are doing business with a reputable dealer, send a money order or a certified check with your order. It takes from ten days to two weeks for personal checks to clear and most shipments will be held until they do. The more valuable the object, the surer you can be of a waiting period.

DON'T ask for things to be sent C.O.D. unless the dealer offers that privilege. Even then, there are many ifs. If you are not at home to receive the package and it has to be returned to the Post Office, if for some reason you fail to pick up the package—maybe you were away, maybe you lost the notice—and the package goes back to the sender, the possibility of breakage rises with every move; shipping is hazardous at best.

DON'T have dolls shipped to you on a money-back guarantee just to appease your curiosity or in order to get reference pictures of them. This is an old game in an old hobby, and news about you will spread quickly. Eventually many fine opportunities and lists will never be offered to you. The names of good customers are generally kept confidential; the names of bad ones are spread about. Dealers need this sort of help from each other.

Auction Buying

DON'T get auction fever. Get to auctions in time to examine the merchandise or, better still, go to the preview, generally held the day before. Ask to look at whatever interests you, make notes on your catalog or in a notebook using the auction numbers, and decide how much you would be willing to pay for each item in a shop. Mark these prices down. Later, right or wrong, stick to your calm judgment.

If you are really interested in an offering, a practiced auctioneer will sense it and the pace of the bidding may get too fast for you to follow. Don't let yourself be confused. Simply ask loudly for an accounting right then and there. A voice interruption will slow down the runaway tactics. Do not raise your hand—that will simply raise the bid even higher.

An auctioneer may be honest or he may not be above making a few extra dollars one way or another. Such a one may have "shills" in the audience, hirelings to push up prices or to buy items he wants for himself and for which he has an outlet among dealers and collectors.

As with all luxury collectibles and whimsy items, dolls are dependent upon specialized desire. Without an official price or published national standards, nothing is worth a dollar more than the highest bidder is willing to pay for it. That is why most auctions are interesting. If the big bidders come, you may go away empty handed, while the owner and the auctioneer are delighted. But if the big money stays away, and you know your field and have saved for the event, it will seem that heaven has opened its doors to you.

What To Look For in Bodies

DON'T buy dolls which are tightly sewed into clothes or whose wigs must be blasted off. Clothing which cannot be removed usually hides someone's patient but inexperienced repairs for a child; mischief in the line of unprofessional repairs, makeshift assemblage of parts; or a deliberate covering of an entirely wrong body. This is true of all kinds of dolls, from cloth-bodied shoulder heads through jointed wooden or composition bodies, bent-leg infants, celluloids, and all-bisques.

Through the entire history of doll production, some firms made complete dolls, some made heads or bodies only. Many old shoulder heads were sold individually and the bodies were made at home with cloth or leather arms and legs or with porcelain arms and legs which could be bought separately.

DON'T buy dolls in special costumes or make-ups unless you undress and examine them critically.

Nuns, peasants, and queens with wimples and veils, for instance, are often elaborately dressed to hide a broken neck, a badly cracked back of a head, or a shoulder head without a shoulder of any kind. These latter are anchored to a body by way of a heavy stick with a ball of string at the top which was soaked in glue and forced into the head while it was soft—an old practice to repair dolls for little girls, but not one acceptable to collectors. Feeling through the headdress is not enough. The doll must be undressed to be sure, for even the present owner may not be aware of it.

Long stockings or kid shoes glued or tightly sewed over china legs may hide repaired or broken feet which cannot be felt through the coverings. Tight sleeves can be used to cover repaired arms if the hands are in good condition.

Arms and legs of celluloids are sometimes held by tight clothing. The biggest handicap of celluloids is the punched holes in the arm and leg sockets which hold the rubber. The original stringing is almost impossible to remove without damaging these sockets and if the holes are enlarged in the process, it is difficult to get a purchase for the new rubber. Sewed-on clothing can hide a multitude of sins!

In all-bisques, it is possible to hide ingenious wire stringing loops, glued torso parts, even wrong arms and legs.

Clowns with elaborately painted faces should be thoroughly examined. Clown faces were produced in both France and Germany, but the buyer should be certain that the make-up was fired on in a porcelain works and is not someone's recent attempt at portraiture to hide a broken face. Quite often the black or red outlines of the new face design or the new additions to the old design follow some of the cracks in the face. Old fired paints will be translucent like the ordinary complexion coating and not opaque; they will also have sunk into the pores of the bisque without leaving an accumulation of paint on the surface. Old fired colors are scrubbable—a point for collectors to remember.

DON'T buy china or bisque shoulder heads which are tightly—often newly—sewn to bodies or glued to bodies, whether the bodies are old or new. Modern porcelain repair can be difficult to distinguish in ordinary light and all or parts of the shoulders and/or heads can be beautifully rebuilt on medical wire cloth. Medical wire cloth comes in many grades and is a sturdy, flexible metal mesh which is ideal for exceptional repairs.

Instead of having the tapes sewn, doll heads with shoulder plate holes should have the tapes in place, but held with small safety pins. Doll heads without shoulder plate holes are more difficult to keep in place, but you should be allowed to examine them before your money changes hands; the underside of the shoulder plate and the inside of the head are definitely your business if you are a serious purchaser. Honest repair artists, often extremely talented, do not want their work to be part of a fraud and usually do not cover the undersides of shoulders or the insides of heads with repair material which exactly resembles porcelain.

Eventually you should learn to spot repairs on close examination, and you will probably buy damaged heads that you can have repaired yourself. But while you are learning, simply insist on knowing what you are buying and only pay for what it is. With a reputable dealer, there may be a difference of several hundred dollars in a rare head which has been repaired and the same head in perfect original condition.

Again, when jointed dolls came into vogue, some firms made complete dolls, some made heads or bodies only and bought the missing units from specialists in the field. There were also doll assemblers who bought all the parts from the same specialists.

Whatever the case, there is a wide variation in the color of bodies even from the same manufacturer and at different periods. The old ones were deep ivory under the varnish. This gradually was changed to the "high" pink or rose color of the late dolls. The parts may all fit reasonably well, but sewed-on clothes can hide an ivory torso with deep rose limbs or parts of limbs and vice versa.

Porcelain repair on medical wire cloth can work wonders with swivel heads as well as the shoulder head types. Many an artist can repair a broken mouth or nose, replace missing parts from an eye socket, chunks out of the top rims, and even the base of a neck so that the doll can be properly restrung without worry about its holding fast.

Porcelain repair is a great help not only to the collector with limited funds who cannot buy perfect dolls, but also to well-to-do collectors who buy repaired objects of all kinds. Museums have used this type of repair for generations. Thanks to such books as *Repairing and Restoring China and Glass,* by William Karl Klein (Harper and Row, 1962) the closely guarded secrets of the repairing trade, passed from father to son, have been made public. (A. Ludwig Klein & Son, of which firm William Karl was a fifth generation member, was founded in Dresden in 1786, and moved to Philadelphia in the early 1900s.)

If you would have a collection instead of a "bunch of dolls," you should be willing to learn how to mend and restring them, how to dress them properly, whether you make the clothes yourself or have someone do it for you. You should keep them clean and presentable—and you should keep adequate records.

Eyes and Wigs

DON'T believe all brown-eyed dolls are "rare." By its very nature brown is a more difficult color to handle than blue. French paperweight blue eyes, whether threaded or feathered, are gorgeous; some of the brown eyes of the same type seem to have a golden quality which is also beautiful. There are ten shades of blue to perhaps three in brown, and the delicate threading or feathering of the tiny threads show to greater advantage in blue. There may be fewer brown-eyed dolls, but they are by no means rare, or even uncommon.

German blown eyes are another story. Because they are blown in exactly the same way as familiar Christmas tree balls, they do not have the clear glass cornea which gives the fabulous depth to French paperweight eyes. The pupil is on the bottom of the ball and the iris surrounds it, with the balance of the eye and the neck made of white glass. Some of the patterns in these blue eyes are very pretty, with dark outer rims, threaded or feathered centers, and large pupils.

Blue lends itself to more designs and shades than brown, and can also be blended with gray to give another group of color tints. For generations Germany produced the finest blue dyes in the world—blue was from the beginning a difficult color to keep stable—and it is little wonder that they made beautifully colored eyes in blue. Besides that, most Anglo-Saxons for whom the dolls were made were blue-eyed, and it seemed normal to provide blue-eyed dolls for blue-eyed children. The fact that Queen Victoria had blue eyes had nothing to do with a shortage of brown eyes.

At this late date a good doll does not need to have the color of her eyes exaggerated in order to promote her sale. Desirable dolls always find a waiting market.

Wigs welded on with gobs of Elmer's Glue have definitely been replaced. The Germans used yellow glue or mucilage; the French tacked wigs into cork domes for many years. Replaced wigs can hide cracked, broken, or mended heads. The buyer is entitled to check the insides of heads for such price-reducing flaws.

Tightly glued wigs often hide German sleep eyes which have been set. While there is nothing dreadfully wrong with professionally set German sleep eyes—and frequently setting improves the doll's appearance—the buyer should know if it has been done.

Many of us who have handled countless sleep-eyed dolls are convinced that in emergen-cies when the manufacturers ran short of the proper size eye, or perhaps as an economy measure when costs were figured in fractions of a cent, the Germans not infrequently used eyes that were too small. Quite often the plaster wafers which hold the eyes in place can be seen protruding into the outside corners of the eye cuts. Sometimes the eyes wobble badly, even though they are original. In other instances, we are sure the heavy waxing of the lids and/or unusually thick eyelashes were used to improve the fit of obviously small sleep eyes.

When dolls are left on their backs for years, eyes often fall out of place. Some dolls were put away in trunks or attics with loose or broken eyes when the child finished with them. Broken eyes must be replaced; loose eyes remounted, rewaxed, and reset.

Simple setting with plaster of Paris is the least expensive repair; some dealers and collectors can do this work themselves without breaking the face when the plaster heats up. When this economy has been practiced, the seller should explain it, and perhaps reflect it in the price. The buyer is entitled to know what method was used on a doll, and a tightly glued wig prevents inspection.

DON'T forget that old dolls had mohair wigs almost without exception. Some were much finer and more beautiful than others, but even the commonest were becoming. An old doll should be sold bareheaded rather than in some harsh, brassy modern wig. Many collectors buy old dolls they really do not want in order to get an old wig in good condition that will fit a cherished doll which is without one. This can be an expensive habit, but a good old wig is a prize indeed.

Dressing Your Doll

DON'T be misled about "original" clothing on dolls. More often it is "as found." Those of us old enough to remember Christmas trips to toy departments of such stores as Wanamaker's and Gimbel Brothers, also remember tilted shelves lined with dolls tied securely in boxes. They were elaborately dressed in frilled bonnets and dresses of the flimsiest kinds of materials, hung with cheap cotton lace. Both material and lace were loaded with filling which did not wear well, and became limp on the first rainy day on the porch. If the clothing had any closures at all, they were infrequent, with thread eyes and cheap hooks that rusted.

The loving gifts of mothers, aunts, and grandmothers who made new clothing regularly as presents for little girls were far superior to factory clothing. Many are fit for a princess, but they are "as found," not "original." A doll that truly still wears its original clothing is generally the sad doll that was never played with.

DON'T pay for gaudy rayon or nylon clothes on an old doll. The majority of old dolls of whatever kind were dressed in cotton or woolen materials; silk was an expensive luxury and dolls were a competitive business in which all corners were cut to the bone. Dolls can be dressed in old silk if it is available, but rayon and nylon are utterly wrong because they are not of the period.

DON'T buy or dress German jointeds as women. They were miniature little girls intended to be the beloved children of real little girls. Except for a few mature "character" faces, German jointeds should be dressed as children in the styles of their own times.

By the same token, chinas and fancy Parians and bisques with elaborate molded hair should be dressed as women, but in their proper periods.

All of which means you should buy yourself some fashion books, either old magazines— these could run to considerable expense, or some of the recent books about dolls' clothes, which present proper attire for each type. Some even provide patterns. Paper dolls of a particular era also offer suggestions.

DON'T waste time trying to prove there is an easier way to go about becoming a collector or dealer, for without patience, study, unending effort and watchfulness, you cannot help but be defeated.

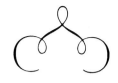

Odds and Ends

Most collectors start by going out to find one very special doll which is either like one they owned as a child or like one they have seen and wanted as a child. A great many of today's advanced collectors originally started with German jointeds and bent-leg infants or all-bisques because they remembered them so pleasantly from their childhoods. They had no idea of ever buying chinas or woodens or waxes which were so very different from the pink-cheeked, open-mouthed, sleep-eyed German products of the late 1890s and early 1900s.

Not many of them were interested in French dolls either, because as children they had never seen a Jumeau with its heavy eyebrows, or a Bru with its puffed cheeks, or a so-called French Fashion representation of an adult. And surely the collectors who have studiously gathered and recorded almost every type of Japanese doll were not originally motivated in that direction.

Collectors' tastes change as their interest in dolls grow, and this is what makes an advanced or a specialized collector. Some types of dolls are an acquired taste, and many women who started with ordinary German dolls are now formidable authorities in other fields which have captured their attention along the way.

The term "antique dolls" covers a multitude of types and should not frighten the beginner. Many of them are not antique at all by the standards set for other collectibles. Until February 1966, the United States Customs had decreed that any antiquity coming into this country must have been made before 1830. The fine French dolls collectors seek so eagerly were made after 1850 and a great many of them, and German as well, came about in the 1890s and later. Under the new customs specifications, the general rule

that an antique must be at least 100 years old is more realistic, and in the next twenty or thirty years, open-mouthed German and French dolls will qualify. They are the most available now and the least expensive in most instances—always a good starting place for anything collectible.

American collectors have been led to believe that the German doll industry was completely destroyed during World War I. Not true! World War I did interrupt both French and German production, but both managed to re-establish production and both manufactured dolls into the next decade. The *Societie Francaise de Fabrication de Bebes et Jouets* (S.F.B.J.), a coalition formed in 1899 to meet German competition, continued into the 1950s. Some German firms lasted, with increasingly poor products, into the era of Occupied Germany.

The Bye-Lo Baby, copyrighted in 1922, was made in Germany, as was E. I. Horsman's delightful competitive infant, copyrighted in 1924. Rose O'Neill's Kewpies were made by the millions in the 1920s with every possible German porcelain works participating in the production.

In the minds of Americans, Dresden is the magic word for porcelain production and it is true that the city of Dresden was completely demolished by British and American air attacks. But that was in World War II, long after the German doll industry had been severely crippled by other world factors.

Japan had jumped into the bisque doll and toy chinaware picture about 1915 when World War I stopped European exports to America. Previous to that time, most of their products had been marked NIPPON; but actively seeking the lucrative American market, they changed it to MADE IN JAPAN. Many of the dolls also bore the name or trademark label of the biggest and most aggressive manufacturer, Morimura Brothers.

Because international patent laws were and still are lax, the molds for the hasty Japanese production were openly taken from identifiable German dolls. Some were changed a little; others not at all. The quality was typically poor, the decorating uncommonly bad, but the prices undercut even the cheapest German products.

A new attitude has entered the doll field with the surge of new collectors from the late teens to the early forties in age. The teens, having had nothing but plastic dolls in their childhood are utterly fascinated by all kinds of old dolls. Their older sisters, more conscious of antiques in general, are close to being experts at furrowing out good quality, well designed, old objects for their homes. Because they are studious rather than impulsive, and are used to operating within a budget, they know exactly what they are looking for when they decide to collect dolls.

Because of these new and variable factors, there are few types of dolls without their own fan clubs. Some women never want anything but German dolls; others switch to French, and keep only early German types. Some collectors look for papier-mâchés, others are in love with rag and cloth dolls. Infants never lose their appeal to many women. There are entire collections of paper dolls, and dealers who specialize in nothing else.

Many women start paying attention to dolls only when they find their own daughters' dolls, forgotten in the attic, and they concentrate entirely on American-made dolls, some dating back to World War I days when the doll market had to meet its needs with any merchandise available. There are collectors who are interested in nothing but Madame Alexander dolls, or movie star creations, or comic characters, or Dionne Quints.

There are absolutely no rules about what dolls anyone must collect. The field is wide open to personal preference and the cost of the dolls is no criteria if the collection is accurate and authentic.

A general collection, housing anything and everything which interests the collector personally, is perhaps the most satisfying and the least frustrating. Without one's heart set upon this or that, with no gaping holes which are impossible to fill, and with favorites in every type and size, the general collector is often the happiest.

She also has the joy of acquiring dolls unexpectedly. She falls in love with a face and she buys the doll, and, just because it is different than any of her others, the real pleasure of ownership lasts a long time. In fact, it never really wears away because the general collector seldom buys duplicates; each doll can be her favorite of that type.

There is one exception to that—the woman who has an overwhelming love for twins. Another version of the same complaint, is to find big and little sisters and brothers. Doll faces change so much as they are reduced in size from the huge original molds that the contrast provides interesting comparisons. "Family resemblances" can become completely fascinating.

What can a collector expect to find in a lifetime? Nobody knows. A great deal depends on the area in which you live, how much purchasing you do outside your own area, how devoted and how studious you are about collecting, amount of money you care to invest, and how lucky you are. "What next?" is an element which enters your life when you decide to collect dolls and lends enchantment to the rest of your years.

By learning to care for dolls, to restring them and to do minor repairs, to keep records, perhaps even learning to make wigs, but surely by sewing for them, you will be kept busy and interested in intervals between new dolls.

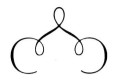

Porcelain Products

In a previous book, *All-Bisque and Half-Bisque Dolls*, (Nelson-National, 1969), the author described in detail the materials, the step-by-step production operations, and the variety of porcelain types. That will not be repeated here.

Briefly, porcelain slip is a soft, thick, creamy white material much like thin pudding. It is composed of clay, fine sand, feldspar, and other carefully proportioned elements. Modern ceramists buy this material ready mixed because they do not have the knowledge of chemistry nor the testing facilities to compound their own mixtures as the German factories seem to have done.

Thick plaster of Paris molds, in two or more parts, absorb the liquid from the slip, and the first step in production is to pour these molds full of slip and allow the slip to set. When the mold is opened the pieces are tender and putty-colored, requiring careful handling. This is the "greenware" stage at which the eye sockets are cut, stringing loops opened, edges straightened, the tops of heads removed if the doll is to have glass eyes, and any seepage removed from the mold seam lines.

All porcelain pieces must be air dried until they have lost all feeling of chill and dampness and have turned pure white, unless the slip was pre-colored to save the coloring operation. These frail pieces are then fired in a kiln (ceramists pronounce this "kill") at a very high temperature and they become quite hard. After they have cooled—a matter of patient waiting no matter what size the kiln—they are hand-sanded until they are quite smooth to the touch. Whatever the abrasive used, the quality of the finished piece depends upon the thoroughness of this sanding process. It is boring, tedious work.

The decorating consists of the application of oil color. In dolls the beautiful pink complexions are done with henna paint which is toned down by "padding" with a ball of lamb's wool in a piece of pure silk or organdy or whatever the processer prefers. The cheeks are "blushed" with an additional application of the same color; blushing is often done on the backs of hands and on the feet if the leg does not have a molded shoe. Eyebrows, eyelashes, if any, the hair, if it is molded, the mouth, and the eye and nose dots are also part of the decorating and difficult to do properly.

Some accomplished artists are able to do several of these operations at one time, thus reducing the number of times the piece must be returned to the kiln for another firing. The beautiful scrubbable finish on bisque is made permanent by the same kind of firing which first turns the slip into porcelain.

To differentiate between types of porcelain products, common names have been given each kind.

Bisque is the word used for the completely colored variety, whether it be a doll, a figurine, a doll head, or a decorative display item.

China is used to indicate anything which has a glazed finish. The word derives from the dishes on your table which are glazed to keep food stains from penetrating the absorbent porcelain base. Glazes vary, but the firing to harden them is done at much lower temperatures to keep the glaze from crazing or cracking. Like bisque, pieces to be glazed are cleaned, fired to porcelain, finished, decorated, allowed to dry thoroughly, glazed, and then low fired.

Parian came into the porcelain vocabulary because of a statuette shown at the Crystal Palace exhibition in London in 1851. Because the product resembled the beautiful marble from the Greek Island of Paros, it was identified as "Parian ware." We have no proof that dolls or doll heads were made of Parian ware but the Germans did make dolls and doll heads of pure white porcelain with only the features and the hair or decorations colored. Doll collectors have borrowed the word to indicate any doll or head which is of extremely high quality, beautifully finished and decorated, but not complexion coated.

Mongrel words have slipped into the doll vocabulary and novices should exercise great care when dolls are described in such terms.

They should also watch out for such pieces with exaggerated descriptions.

Sugar or *salt bisque* are two examples of this inaccurate terminology. These are generally applied to dolls or heads which are not complexioned but which are definitely NOT Parian. Everything good is imitated and these were originally cheap doll creations made for no better purpose than to follow the trend or to avoid the increased expense of the complexioning which also required an additional trip to the kiln. In many instances, too, these dolls appear to be seconds or even actual discards of the factories which originally created them.

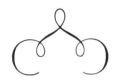

China Heads

Novices are rarely attracted to chinas unless they have inherited a grandmother's or even a great-grandmother's doll. Even then, with the collecting spark ignited, the pink loveliness of the French and even the German jointeds appeals to them as they tour the antiques circuit. Until collectors have put in some mileage, too, the prices of chinas with elaborate hairdos, glass eyes, and the like, appalls them. And rightly so.

It cannot be said often enough that all collectors, new and advanced, should study and look before whipping out their checkbooks. There are some unusual chinas which any well-informed collector would enjoy possessing, but the word "rare" should be dropped from the doll vocabulary. The collector should know at first sight if a doll is uncommon, but it should not be called "rare" just to arouse interest.

The average collector is inclined to be neat, and the bodies on many chinas repel the novice. Stained and often rotting from sheer age, filled with all kinds of concoctions from bran through cotton, hair, and animal hair, they frequently are unlovely sights. Many have kid arms that are sometimes a complete horror, and fat, stuffed legs with sewed-on shoes that do not seem to be appropriate. Even worse, if they originally had nice china arms and legs, one of each is broken or missing, or all four are just stumps. It is discouraging, to say the least. All remnants of the old bodies should be kept, however, even if the head must be put on a new body.

Like olives, china heads are an acquired taste, but it helps to know some of the common and desirable points about chinas so that a good china will not be overlooked.

Many dollers think a collection is incomplete without a few china examples, including the common ones. Common dolls are poor investments though. It is wise to purchase them only for the pleasure that collecting them can bring. Common dolls are easy to obtain, because collectors have a natural tendency to try to sell their more ordinary dolls to pay for finer ones. Prices on these dolls should be in keeping with their availability and quality.

Age is usually an important factor in judging a china, but among the molded-hair dolls one must know more than hair styles to date them properly. Manufacturers used the same molds as long as dolls sold well. Also, they could reach back in time to select a hairdo without breaking any rules. Because dolls were toys, nobody took them seriously except to make money on them and to keep the porcelain factories busy all year round.

Dollers should also remember that a talented modern artist can reproduce any hair style and decorating technique.

No. 1 The most available of all chinas has acquired three interchangeable names to identify it—low brow, 1880 hairdo, and common head. This china with its round shaped head has smooth waves instead of molded curls, and a short neck which adds to the youthful appearance. The doll loses much of her charm when compared to the elegant lady chinas of an earlier time. She is 12 inches tall and has a slightly worn cloth body, the color of burnt orange. It is stuffed with sawdust. The bisque arms are shaped so that they may be used interchangeably as left and right, improving the chances of replacing a missing one. The fat legs have threaded ridges and glazed brown shoes. The heels of the shoes are another indication that the doll is from a later period. She has two sew holes and the word

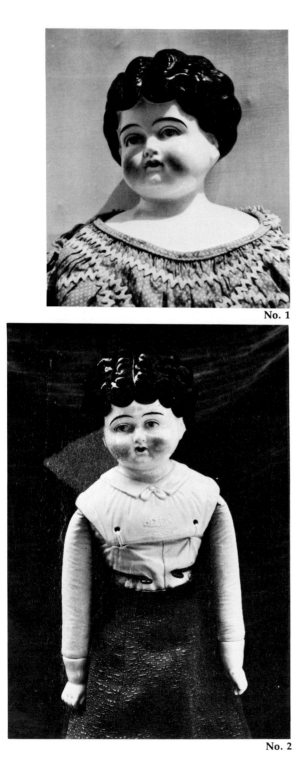

No. 1

No. 2

Germany faintly incised on the shoulder. This particular china was a survivor of a tornado in 1914; a nail then driven through the body remains today.

Black was the most popular hair color, but more blondes were made with the low-brow hairstyle than any other. This should also be considered when purchasing a blond common head china.

The term "1880 china" is especially misleading for a new collector. A study of various wholesale catalogs reveals that the hair style was mass produced in the 20th century. In 1925, the regulation china limb dolls with this hairdo were advertised for $3.25 per dozen by the wholesaler, Butler Brothers.

No. 2 The name chinas of the 20th century also have the 1880 hair style. Most advanced collectors consider that a name painted in gold adds little to quality or value. The Butler Brothers advertisement regarding the name chinas stated: "Our well known trademark Pet Name is in the mold and cannot be effaced." In 1908, the Pet Name dolls were described as having molded necklaces. However, in another section of the catalog the same name heads were described as having a collar with a bow, which is more accurate. It is frustrating for the modern researcher to learn that the descriptions in the catalog were not always correct or complete. There was always a tendency to exaggerate claims. Examination of dolls remains a vital part of research.

The Pet Name dolls must have been well received. For more than 25 years Butler Brothers marketed these Pet Name dolls. In 1916, Marion, Agnes, Helen, Bertha, Dorothy, and Ethel were the names listed. The doll pictured is a "Helen." As late as 1931, Butler Brothers advertised the 12½-inch size for $2.

Chinas with printed cloth bodies were also popular in the early part of the 20th century. The ABC printed cloth bodies advertised in *Our Drummer* catalog not only have letters of the alphabet but words with drawings of objects beside the word. In 1916, Butler Brothers sold the 10-inch dolls for $1.20 per dozen. The advertising claim that these were educational is perhaps true. The technique is remarkably similar to the modern work books used in the first grade.

No. 3 An 11-inch blond china, this doll has a

printed cloth body which features the multiplication tables and objects with their names printed underneath. The colors found on the body are red, blue, green, black, and yellow on a beige background. The illustrations include a horse, cart, hare, drum, strawberries, and other objects. The bisque legs have dark brown, glazed shoes, but no ridges. The Roman numeral **VII** is a size number on each leg. The legs are still tacked together to keep them from breaking. Incised on the back of the right shoulder is **4 Germany**. There are no sew holes.

The illustrated cloth bodies with a wide range of subjects, toys, flowers, and storybook characters often show more imagination and artistry than the common heads. These dolls are still within reach of the beginning collector. Occasionally they can be purchased for the same price as a common head china with a less interesting body.

No. 4 There are always exceptions to any generalized axiom. It is not always true that hair style determines the value of a china, or that early chinas are better than late ones. An open mouth china with teeth has the low brow hair style but is regarded as a choice doll. The teeth are molded, not glued, in the mouth. All indications are that the doll is a late example; the chubby arms and legs are a late style, as is the face decoration. Dollers have been quick to label chinas with teeth as rare. However, such a doll was advertised as a special bargain by Butler Brothers in 1908. There is little question that is is a china, because in the sketch the hair style can be recognized as low brow, and the ad described the doll as "Glazed, good size china heads." The words "open mouth with teeth" are printed in heavier type. On the illustrated body is a design called "Flags of All Nations." The prices ranged from 69 cents a dozen to $1.87 for a half dozen of the 17-inch size. Just because a doll was advertised by a national wholesaler does not mean it was common, but the supply probably was more plentiful than is often assumed, because outlets were advised to "Buy these goods and sell them close as we have done." This high-volume, low-profit method of selling would not be practical with a limited amount. Collectors would like to know what happened to these bargain dolls.

No. 5 A, B, C The word "rare" is frequently attached to china bonnets, but it is not always

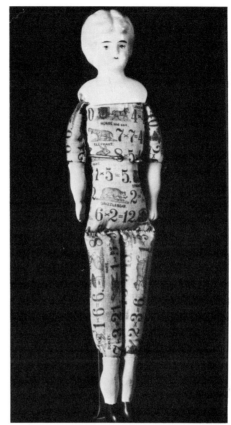

No. 3

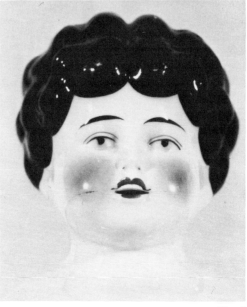

No. 4

No. 5A   No. 5B   No. 5C

correct. Bonnet style **No. 5 A** has been found in collections in all parts of the country, usually decorated in the same colors. The rim of the bonnet is orange brown, with a pale lavender bow. The molded ruffles on the bonnet are indistinct. Perhaps this indicates the mold was poor or worn from use. The back of the head is simply glazed white. Waves similar to the common or so-called 1880 hairdo are revealed beneath the bonnet. The eyes are painted blue with such large pupils that at first glance she appears to be a black-eyed china. Under the chin is a pale blue bow, economically painted with one horizontal stroke of the brush and two diagonal ones. While not rare, she is an interesting addition to a collection. The same style appeared as a blonde **(5 B, C).**

No. 6 Compared to No. 5, this blond bonnet head is superior. The ruffles surrounding the face and bow at the chin are quite detailed. The

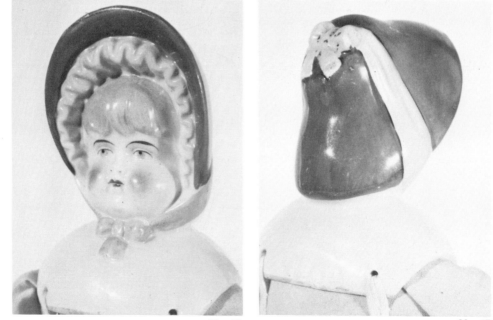

No. 6A   No. 6B

No. 7

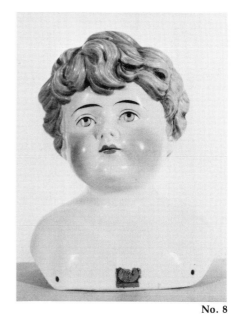

No. 8

blond hair and the face are nicely decorated. Also, the back of the bonnet is decorated, requiring more time and expense to make.

No. 7 Because they are most noticeable in dolls with black hair, this "Highland Mary" (also known as "Currier & Ives") is a good example of a desirable china with brush strokes. Instead of painting an even line around the hair edges on the forehead and at the temples, the artist very likely drew a brush over the molded hairline to give this attractive finish. The lines are so fine they appear to be from a drying brush rather than from a newly dipped one. Under a magnify-

ing glass, brush marks can also be seen on the blond head, but the effect is nearly lost on the yellow hair. Both are from the 1870s.

No. 8 Comb marks are difficult to illustrate but they are threadlike lines molded in the hair which give the impression that a comb has been passed over it. The nicest comb marks are across the crowns of dolls whose hair would be considered straight but they were frequently used in curls to add texture to the painted hair, as in this illustration.

No. 9 A, B This broken doll is a good example of parted lips, as well as several other charac-

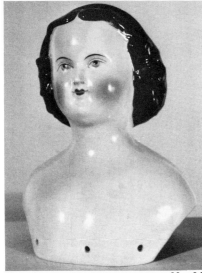

No. 9A

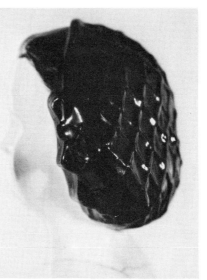

No. 9B

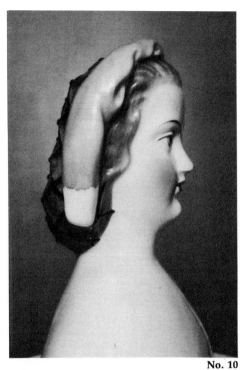

No. 10

No. 11

teristics. She shows the red eyelid lines and the high placement of her pupils, which is typical of the older dolls. A reproduction artist can duplicate both features without much trouble; consequently they should not be the only points considered in judging chinas.

By her left eye and high on her forehead there are samples of "pitting," and on her neck she has "freckling." Both of these are evidence that the doll is old; modern slip is so good that these disfigurements have been eliminated. They are specks of foreign matter which, because they were heavier than the clay in the slip, fell through until they were stopped by the walls of the plaster of Paris mold. Unfortunately, the impurities were on the surface of the doll and marred her beauty. We have no way of knowing whether they decreased the price of the heads in their own day but, with the passion for perfection that exists now, they can sometimes delay the sale of a doll.

With all this, she also has another problem—her name. In some areas she is called "Nancy Hanks with bows and a snood," but occasionally she turns up as "Mary Todd Lincoln with bows and a snood." Quite a few other chinas have several names. How these names became attached to them is unknown, but they are here to stay.

The side view of the same doll shows the snood molded right into the hair to imitate the knotted silk hairnets fashion periodically decreed for women. The snood lines were sometimes picked up in a color or in gold, but most often were colored with the hair. The molded bows at the ears and the band across the head also show up well.

No. 10 An oldie named "Eugenia," with snood and headband, whose pert little oval face, parted lips, and eye treatment indicate that she is much older than the average china.

No. 11 Exposed ears in chinas were sometimes pierced through lobes, as in this love-worn lady. She may have been decorated over the glaze, which would account for the washed-out features, or perhaps the fact that she was much played with, indicated by the worn hair, may have contributed to her faded look.

No. 12 A, B With her molded curls in front and bow in back, this is an interesting head but

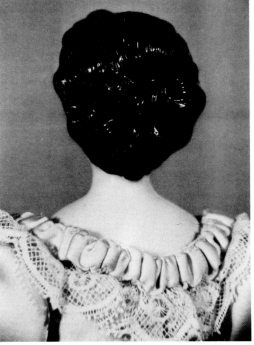

No. 12A

No. 12B

because it is black much of the elaborateness is lost.

No. 13 "Dagmar" suffers from the same complaint. Dagmar is another black haired china with a front molded band and bow which is difficult to illustrate. In fact, they are difficult to see, even when you have the doll in hand. The band reappears out from under the side puffs and extends across the back of the head above a double row of short curls which are molded low on the neck.

No. 14 A, B Even those who do not enjoy chinas are usually impressed with this magnificient Dresden porcelain doll head. Her elaborate hairdo has windblown bangs and delicate tendrils which fall about her ears and cheeks. On top of her head the hair is gathered into soft swirls. The brown hair, a rare color, is painted a second time with a darker brown to represent hair strands. Instead of the usual one-stroke eyebrows she has the feathered eyebrows which have a more natural appearance. The incised eyes looking to the side are rarely seen in a china, and are pleasing. Painted lower eyelashes are another unusual feature. Her smiling lips are parted, showing a suggestion of painted teeth. Another desirable point is her slender neck

No. 13

No. 14A

No. 14B

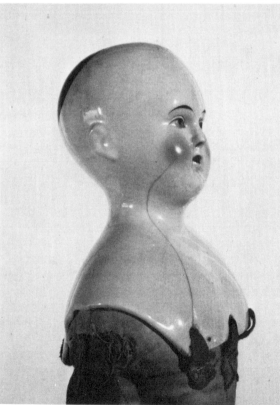

No. 15

which has a throat hollow. She is wearing an ormolu and glass necklace, made especially for dolls.

No. 15 A china with a bald head is often called a Biedermeier, but the word actually does not identify or date the doll. The doll has blue eyes with a fine red painted line above the black outlined lid. Black pupils with a white highlight beside it touch the upper eyelid. Red dots are found at the nostrils and corners of the eyes; the cheeks are very rosy, the lips are painted with upturned corners, indicating a smile. Originally; the doll had a wig which covered the painted black spot on top of the head.

No. 16 The bangs and brush strokes at the temples add to the appeal of this black haired doll. But the large brown eyes are a feature which would attract the most attention from collectors.

No. 17 Another brown-eyed girl has a flat top hair style associated with the dolls of the Civil War era. Other desirable qualities include comb marks, white center part, and detailed ears.

No. 18 Even more unusual, this doll which also has a flat top hair style with center part, exposed ears and brown eyes, has rare lower eyelashes painted with a precise stroke.

No. 19 These blond and black-haired girls have the same massive curls and tousled bangs. An example with identical hair style, once

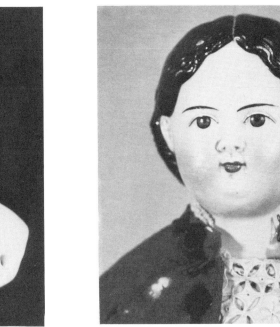

No. 16

No. 17

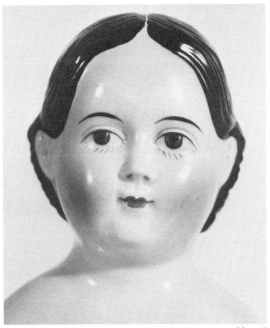

No. 18

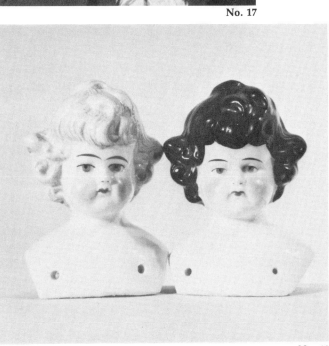

No. 19

owned by Robert E. Lee's daughter, is on display at the museum in Lexington, Virginia.

No. 20 Charles Dotter patented the idea of a printed corset on a doll body. The head found on most recognizable Dotter bodies is incised under the glaze **Pat. Dec. 7/80** and sometimes the size figure appears under the mark. We have no way of knowing whether every head so marked was originally used on a Dotter body. It is possible that production overages or seconds could have been sold as separate heads or on bodies of other manufacturers. If only the head survives, it is best to label it as a Dotter-type.

Unfortunately, Mr. Dotter used a poor grade of cotton material for his doll bodies, and the corset was printed only on the front portion. The bodies now, if they have not fallen apart completely, are often in deplorable condition, unfit to dress or display. If the arms and legs are intact and some portions of the printed torso remain, a new body can be made and the ragged bits of the original body basted in place. A further method of preservation is to cover the entire body with net before the head is reglued. In this way, the collector has some evidence to prove that the head was originally used by Dotter.

No. 21 The Ruth Gibbs dolls which were formerly made in Flemington, New Jersey, are beginning to attract the attention of collectors although the dolls rarely appear in print. The 7-inch china illustrated often was sold as one of the "Little Women." Ruth Gibbs obtained a copyright in 1948 for "Ruth Gibbs Godey's Lady Book Dolls," stating that she had used the name since 1946. In 1950, another trademark was obtained for "Godey's March Family" to represent the dolls inspired by the characters of Louisa May Alcott. Although these dolls are very late in comparison to other chinas they should not be classified as reproductions. The dolls do not imitate older ones. The distinctive painting style includes eyelashes, heart-shaped mouth, and sometimes colors of red and blond hair not found on the older dolls. The molded shoes have tiny heels and are a gold color. The stuffed bodies are a light pink color, closely matching the tinted shade of the china. Many Gibbs dolls are incised with a faint **R** and **G**. At the moment they are inexpensive, but the Gibbs dolls may be sleepers.

No. 20

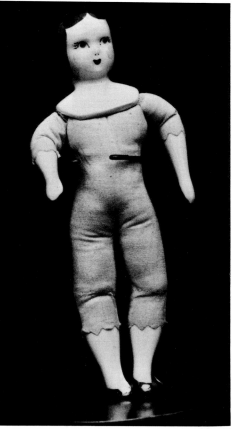

No. 21

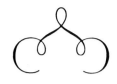

French Dolls
with Bisque Heads

For years collectors have predicted that French dolls would shortly peak in value. To the despair of the beginning collector, the increase in prices has continued at a startling rate. But little money to spend on dolls does not always mean that an excellent example is unobtainable.

At a flea market in Portugal, one alert collector discovered a dirt-caked bisque head resting on the ground. Upon examining it she was amazed to discover it was a closed mouth Bru, one of the most sought-after of all French dolls. She bought it for $10. At that time a collector would normally be expected to pay in the neighborhood of $1,500 for a doll of this quality. The fact that this did not happen in the early 1950s but in the summer of 1971 is encouraging. There are still bargains in the doll world.

Société Française Bébé et Jouets

Traditionally, the French dolls were expensive until four of the barely surviving firms combined, in 1899 to help meet the aggressive German competition. Strangely, the German firm, Fleischman & Blodel, was included as a fifth member. Other companies joined later. The new combine was called *Société Française Bébés et Jouets* (Corporation of French Manufacturers of Dolls and Toys).

For convenience, collectors use the initials **S.F.B.J.** Because the prices of French dolls were decreased by the corporation, some French dolls marked **S.F.B.J.** remain in the price range of the collector with limited funds. The quality in many of these dolls is a poor second to the earlier ones, but an inexpensive S.F.B.J. helps quench the thirst for a French doll.

Some dealers have a habit of referring to S.F.B.J. by the name of one of the earlier firms, such as Jumeau. An additional source of confusion was that the trademarks **Bru, Jumeau** and **Eden Bébé** were sometimes used by S.F.B.J. It is wise to check every mark personally.

No. 22 This pretty 12-inch mulatto girl of Martinque is a good example of the less expensive **S.F.B.J.** Her painted bisque is light brown with slight cheek color. For economy, the manufacturer kept the decorating to a minimum. The

No. 22

stationary black eyes lack the familiar red dots found at the corners. Also, there are no eyelashes. She has one-stroke eyebrows and red dots at the nostrils. The open mouth has molded teeth and the lips are a pleasing rose.

The composition body, painted the same brown as the face, jointed only at the hips and shoulders, is an economy touch. Although this doll is not an expensive type, her legs and arms are well shaped. Another economy touch is her painted black boots. The word **Martinque** is printed on the factory clothing of colorful cotton. Her over-skirt of navy with a white and red print creates a slightly mystic touch. Although her ears are not pierced, one circle earring is sewed in her black mohair wig.

For collectors the character dolls of S.F.B.J. have great appeal. However, they are more expensive.

No. 23 An **S.F.B.J.** doll has a different look due to the curly molded hair and black glass eyes. The mouth with molded teeth has an almost paper-thin opening. The head is marked **Unis.**

No. 24 An infant with a happy expression, incised **S.F.B.J. 236,** has brown sleeping eyes and an open/closed mouth, two molded teeth.

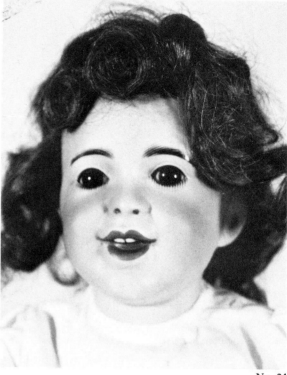

No. 24

The nice quality bisque head has an open crown covered by a mohair wig. The double chin and prominent ears add to the character look. The bent-leg composition is typical of bodies that became popular in the second decade of the 20th century.

French Fashions

Prior to the middle 1870s, most of the dolls made were ladies with closed mouths and narrow waists. Collectors have applied the misleading term "French Fashion" to this type of doll. Because the wardrobes of the fashions were so elaborate, it is easy to understand why collectors thought the dolls were designed to model the latest styles. Actually, the haughty ladies were playthings for rich children.

The term "French Fashion" is used in this book to distinguish these dolls from the many variations of lady dolls. At the moment there is less demand for the once sought-after French Fashions with their stylized faces. It is not unusual for a collector to pay several hundred dollars for a good example, but the prices of French Fashions seem almost stable when compared to other French dolls.

No. 23

The manufacturers of French Fashions are often difficult to determine because the dolls are basically similar and generally unmarked. Occasionally a Fashion is discovered with a name stamped on the kid body or incised on the head or shoulder.

No. 25 This unmarked Fashion doll has several exquisite costumes, including a two-piece dress made of rose silk and blue wool. Among her accessories are a variety of bonnets made of velvet, straw, and wool, trimmed with ribbon.

This true lady also owns a lace shawl, a fur muff, two pairs of stockings, handkerchiefs, and a tennis racket. Her coronet adds the finishing touch of elegance.

No. 26 A Fashion with an interesting smile has a wooden articulated body which is rare.

No. 27 Not all French Fashions were originally dressed in elaborate costumes. Also unmarked, this example wears original outfit typical of provincial France. The cross is also original.

No. 25

No. 27

No. 26

No. 28

No. 29

No. 28 The original clothing is the best feature of this 15 inch Jumeau Fashion. **No. 29** is another example of a fashion in original clothing.

Established in 1843, the Jumeau dolls spanned a full century. The firm was a success in mass production. In 1882, Jumeau manufactured 85,000 dolls. He increased his production 30 percent the next year; in 1884, he made an impressive 200,000 dolls. As late as the 1950s, dolls were made bearing the honored name of Jumeau. Considering the quantity of dolls that were produced, most Jumeaux should not be labeled as rare dolls. Unfortunately for the collector with limited funds, perfect Jumeaux are almost unobtainable.

Jumeau products had heads of German origin until the Franco-Prussian War of 1870. The firm then became the first French factory to make heads. It did not hesitate to influence young customers in favor of French products. A booklet placed in Jumeau boxes between 1880 and 1884, entitled *Letter of a Jumeau Baby to her Little Mother*, reveals the bitterness of the time. "Camelotte! [Trash]. . . It is good only for those frightful German babies, . . . with their stupid faces of waxed cardboard." An illustration in the booklet shows the Jumeau baby breaking her German rival.

Dolls with red brush strokes on the head are sometimes considered Jumeau. The red marks identified the porcelain decorator who was paid on a piece work basis. This was not an unusual practice. Similar marks can be found on the inside of some old china heads, and also on the backs of fine tableware of all kinds, and on art objects.

No. 30 This small lady has red marking on the back of the head. Her swivel neck, an invention of a rival firm but used by Jumeau, dates her after 1861. This bisque has impurities, a problem that was later eliminated. The decoration is typical of the French Fashions—delicate multi-stroke eyebrows and upper and lower eyelashes. Her small rose mouth has little personality or expression. The machine-stitched kid body has the narrow waist and well developed buttocks divided by three seams. Wafer joints at the hips, knees, and elbows give the body mobility. The fingers of the leather hands are individually stitched and wired.

No. 31 This is a closeup of an eye known as a

French paperweight. With such eyes the pupil and iris are prepared and then clear glass, resembling the human cornea, is applied. This shapes the front similar to the curve of the human eye. The pupil is back in the eye, behind clear glass. The paperweight eyes with a solid blue iris in this early example of the type are small in proportion and lack the natural look of the later eyes. With the addition of a varigated color of the iris, the paperweights achieve beauty and realism.

It is easy to discover whether or not a doll's eyes are true paperweights by holding the doll sideways. If a dome of clear glass extends from the pupil and the colored iris, then the eyes are paperweight. The term "paperweight" is appropriate since paperweights have similar depth through clear glass to the base ornament. Because of the curved shape, paperweight eyes are always stationary.

Emil Jumeau's invention of the ball-jointed body had a more dramatic effect on the doll world than the development of the paperweight eyes. Now there were not only haughty ladies, but dolls that resembled beautiful little girls. Although the German firms were quick to develop their own ball-jointed bodies, there are some basic differences. The old French-type bodies are a pale yellow. The Jumeau bodies also have cinnamon specks in the varnish finish. The French bodies have a heavier childlike sturdiness than their German rivals; wrists of the earlier ones are unjointed and the hands and fingers are thicker than the German.

The German bodies have a decidedly pinker cast, jointed wrists, and spindly fingers which are easily damaged. Some bodies from Germany resemble the French style, however. A widely held theory is that French firms occasionally had German bodies made to French specifications.

No. 32 With the exception of the long-faced doll and the mechanical, the Jumeau incised with **EJ** is the most highly prized. Although not much earlier than some of the Tête Jumeau, the "E J" has a very different look. The incised doll with its fatter cheeks and closed mouth resembles a character. The pale bisque of the "E J" is of better quality but the paperweight eyes have yet to achieve perfection. The normal-size eyes appear to be simply a good threaded example; the iris is still a solid color but with white threadlike lines.

No. 30

No. 31

No. 32

(47)

Until the doll is turned to the side, there is no evidence of depth. Her eyes have a staring and artificial look.

An interesting feature of the decorating is a dark rim around the eyes. Also, the feathered eyebrows are painted with upward strokes, slanted toward the temple. The applied ears with deep canals are a desirable feature. The doll, marked **E J** appeals to collectors because it is a product of excellent quality. Also, this mark can be proven as an early mark.

The booklet that accompanied the Jumeau dolls in the early 1880s stated: "All Jumeau babies carry the name Jumeau, in full, on the back." It is assumed the incised mark **E J** was discontinued. The mark **Tête** (head) **Jumeau** is found on both open- and closed-mouth dolls. It does not mean that Jumeau heads were used on bodies of other manufacturers. The mark was used for decades on dolls of varying quality.

No. 33 This ball-jointed, swivel-neck child has exquisite brown paperweight eyes, closed mouth, and pierced ears. A golden red wig is nailed to her cork pate. The painted upper and lower eyelashes are longer than the "E J" and more delicate than the German. Her multi-stroke eyebrows almost meet at the nose. But her real beauty comes from her lustrous eyes. Her height is 24 inches. Her stamped mark is:

TÊTE JUMEAU
BTE   S.G.D.G.
10
vy

No. 34 Another Tête Jumeau is still dressed in her original pale pink dress.

No. 35 A, B An experienced collector would recognize the origin of the Jumeau Bébé without checking her marks. This mechanical Jumeau would surprise many dollers, since she does not have the "Jumeau look." At first glance she appears to be an Oriental, but closer examination reveals African features. Her adult face of yellow bisque is oval and smaller in proportion to her body than the typical Jumeau. Her black, slanted, narrow eyes are quite a departure from the large expressive paperweights. The arched multi-stroke eyebrows heighten the exotic effect. The closed mouth is unusually full, with a faint suggestion of a smile. On a tray she carries a tea

No. 33

No. 34

No. 35A

No. 35B

service. If her mechanism were still in working order, she would go through the motions of serving tea. The costume of satin and brocade seems too elaborate for a servant. The narrow jewelled slippers complete the unusual look. This doll may safely be classified as rare.

Emil Jumeau spent a vast amount of money displaying his dolls at exhibits all over the world, in advertising to the trade where he publicized his numerous medals and awards, and in printed labels and boxes used for shipping dolls. It isn't apparent that he economized anywhere. Since Jumeau apparently took such pride in his work, it is puzzling that so many obviously Jumeau heads are unmarked.

The answer seem to lie in the attitude a perfectionist could be expected to take toward dolls. There was no possible way for Jumeau to have operated even a limited quantity production without having imperfect heads turn up in every firing of the kilns. Because the mistakes made in the firing process couldn't be altered, common sense and general manufacturing procedures would suggest that:

1. Perfect heads were stamped for the much publicized factory-dressed Jumeau dolls.
2. Heads with minor flaws were stamped and sold in the familiar gauze chemise, instead of the elaborate clothes.
3. Those with kiln cracks in the rims or back of the ears, or chipping which would not show under a wig, were left unstamped and sold to doll assemblers and doll dressing firms.
4. Seriously damaged heads were destroyed.

The *Letter of a Jumeau Baby to her Little Mother* confirms that dolls were inspected and sometimes destroyed:

"He [our maker] examines us with most scrupulous attention. . . . Woe to the unhappy one which does not answer to his expectations, it is pitilessly sent back to the factory with those terrible words: 'Destroy immediately'."

In order to maintain this flexible policy, it would be absolutely necessary NOT to incise the heads, a process done in the original molding. Removing incised marks in mass production would present a formidable problem and a high percentage of unavoidable breakage as the bisque thinned under grinding wheels.

This could easily be the practical reason for the stamping rather than the incising of Jumeau heads. It would also explain why so many obviously Jumeau heads were not stamped; frequently, one or more flaws can be detected in them. The dark separation lines behind the ears, or the fine kiln flaws in the neck holes and the rims are visible even to the inexperienced eye. Henna-colored paints with an oil base are used to tint the complexion, and this oil paint seeps into the tiniest crack or flaw and, as the oil burns off in the firing process, turns into a dark stain which cannot be removed.

Practiced observation also reveals lopsided mouths, eyes, and eyebrows; occasional ears that are not completely pierced to accept earrings; poorly done eyelashes. Sometimes combinations of these defects give a doll a fascinating childlike appearance which appeals to a collector, but factory inspectors were interested only in perfect heads and degrees of perfection.

There was no reason for Jumeau not to sell unmarked heads, and he advertised that he did. In 1892 Jumeau advertised dressed and undressed dolls at discounts ranging from 20 to 40 percent *but not bearing the Jumeau name.* (Coleman, D., M., & M., pg 41.) This could have been an economic necessity due to the flood of German dolls which were entering the world markets.

No. 36 Jumeau made a doll with an adult body which came in a marked and unmarked version. This example, without marks, has an open mouth, blue-gray paperweight eyes, pierced ears, and the typical Jumeau style of decoration. Her hourglass figure places her in the less common category.

How should such dolls be catalogued? It is always best to list a doll exactly as it is, i.e., "unmarked Jumeau-like head on . . ." and then describe the type of body, listing any marks or unusual construction.

Another group of dolls difficult to classify have heads from Germany and marked Jumeau bodies. This practice must have been financially successful because so many of these authenticated dolls have come to light through the years. We can only guess, but the supposition is that they were made for the tourist trade.

In the Gay Nineties and into this century before World War I, wealthy Americans appeared on an annual schedule at the fashionable French resorts. It is unthinkable that these

No. 36

parents would not bring back dolls and toys for the children who had been left at home with governesses. German doll faces appealed to Americans. Even if a choice were offered, it is likely they would select the popular blond, pink-cheeked, blue-eyed doll face which was also supposed to represent the "typical American child." These German faces are strikingly similar to the calendar art of the period as well as the paper dolls, advertising cards, and magazine illustrations.

The fact that the families usually referred to these personal imports as "the French doll" or "the doll that Gramma brought from Paris" adds weight to the contention that dolls were purchased for their personal appeal to the buyer and without any emphasis on the manufacturer. These German heads on French bodies undoubtedly offered a price advantage to visiting Americans and the price helped at Customs when it had to be added to the cost of the expensive dresses from famous Paris salons which the ladies could not resist.

Nobody cared who made a doll. In fact, the wigs were glued on so securely that until it was necessary to replace a wig most people didn't know there was a name on the back of a doll head. Adults referred to a doll by the store from which it was purchased, or by the name of the donor. Children gave them fancy storybook names.

Such dolls should be catalogued by the German maker's name and number with "on a marked Jumeau body". Any authentic information about its origin can be included.

Jumeau also made contract heads which bore the mark of the customer. The beautiful **B.L.** or **Bébé Louvre** doll which was sold by the Paris department store of the same name has long been considered a Jumeau product. At a distance Bébé Louvre greatly resembles a typical Jumeau; on close inspection the painted eyelashes are more numerous.

The Jumeau and S.F.B.J. Connection

When *Societe Francaise Bébé & Jouets* was formed, the trademarks of the earlier firms were

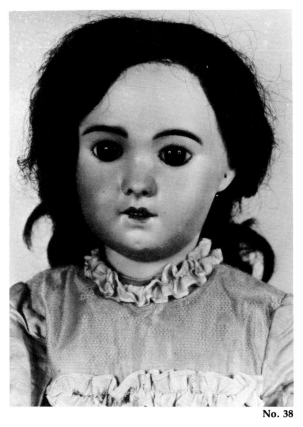
No. 38

retained and later renewed. The older marks were sometimes used without the accompanying S.F.B.J. initials.

No. 37 The S.F.B.J. girl with sleeping eyes is a poorer quality than older dolls. She has ridged eyebrows, a later feature. The holes for pierced ears are so small it appears an earring could not be used. This doll, made of highly colored bisque, has an open mouth molded teeth. Her painted lower eyelashes are straight parallel lines instead of the slanting strokes of earlier Jumeau style decorating. The upper eyelashes are of a material which resembles hair. The mark on the back of her head, **S.F.B.J. 301 Paris**, would not confuse a collector. The body is less sturdy and reminds a collector of German bodies.

No. 38 The doll looks as if it were made from the same mold as **No. 37**. The decorating style is the same—highly colored bisque, and ridged eyebrows. As one would expect, her incised mark is **S.F.B.J. 301 Paris**. But she also has the stamped red mark **Tete Jumeau**.

No. 39 appears to be the same doll as **Nos. 37** and **38**. The sleeping eyes, the ridged brows, straight eyelashes, and high coloring are present.

No. 37

No. 39

Her mouth is open, with molded teeth. She has the two holes in the back of her neck through which strings to tie the eyes protruded. This simple safeguard on sleep-eyed dolls reduced breakage in shipment. It is also a feature found only on later dolls. The body has jointed wrists and thinner proportions. It has a talking mechanism. When the two pull cords are jerked, the doll originally said "Papa" and "Mama", now it makes only an indistinct sound. The only mark on the doll is **Dep. Tete Jumeau**.

The as found clothing has charm.

No. 40, A, B Another interesting doll has the incised mark **Jumeau 1938 Paris**. The controversy concerning whether a series number means the year a doll was made has not been settled. Even without the date, this 32-inch doll appears to be later than any doll discussed in this chapter. Her head has the smooth feel of modern bisque instead of the slightly grainy sensation of the old bisque. The eyebrows are pencil thin, reminiscent of the style popular in the 1930s. The

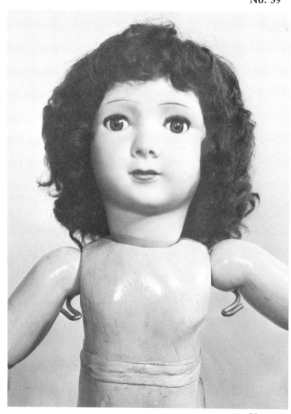

No. 40A

No. 40B

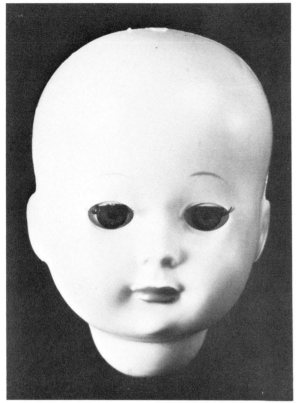

No. 41

painted lower eyelashes are again straight lines. Her lips are a bright red color not found on older dolls. The ears are unpierced. Since dolls follow the fashion of the adult world, this may be an important clue; pierced ears lost favor in the early 20th century. The style did not return until after Jumeau dolls were out of production.

The last of the bisque dolls bearing the Jumeau name seem to have been painted bisque. The term "painted bisque" means that the decorating is done after the bisque has been fired. This bisque color is not as natural and has a tendency to peel and flake. These Jumeaux were made with both open and closed mouths.

No. 41 The last Jumeau made probably was a late celluloid. On the back of the neck is the name **Jumeau** in raised letters. The eyelashes are a modern synthetic material. The eyebrows are made with one stroke, and the lips are bright red. The shape of the mouth is similar to **No's. 40 A** and **B** the 32-inch Jumeau. The head, made in two pieces, is poorly glued behind the ears. The best feature of the head is the name **Jumeau.**

Jumeau was in partnership with a man named Belton for several years. Although there is

much documented information concerning the house of Jumeau, there is little information about Belton. His role in creating dolls remains one of the unsolved mysteries of the doll world. A doll marked "Belton" has never been discovered, and yet the name Belton is used to describe a specific kind of doll.

Belton & Jumeau was a listed firm in 1845. They exhibited in 1844, but by 1847 they had separated. By himself, M. Belton advertised only "dressed dolls" and it was for "dressed dolls" that he won his exhibit prizes. This implies he made clothing and not dolls. No factory address is given in the old directories—only an address for a shop. After he died his wife continued the work for a while. At that time it would have been unusual for a woman to manage a big doll factory.

A personal theory of the authors of this book is that Belton thought of the idea for the closed head, flat on top, which would stand in the kiln on its own top, perhaps held only by a peg of some kind through one of the holes to space the heads properly. Heads that stood upright on their own tops would take up far less room in the kiln than conventional heads.

Either Belton did not patent it (if the idea was his), or he did and the record is lost. But the idea was widely adopted. This we know from the quality of the bisque used, the type of decorating, the coloring, and the number of holes in the tops. The rather coarse heads with the pink eyeshadowing and the small holes are considered French; the very, very fine bisque which is pure white with only the tinted cheeks and with the goatskin wigs like the early Jumeaux, Steiners, and Brus may be early French ones. The heads of medium quality bisque with the larger holes and different decorating may be German. It is probable that untold numbers of "French" heads were manufactured by the highly experienced German porcelain works for French doll manufacturers.

No. 42 This is a Belton-type doll, of very fine pure white bisque with a goatskin wig and lovely French eyes.

No. 43 In center another one of coarser white bisque has pretty eyes, but she is interesting because of the original body. The wooden torso is hand-carved and unpainted. The wooden fingers and toes are only notched, like axe work, and are painted with no attempt to match body color.

No. 42

No. 43

Generally Belton-type are found on French bodies that have chunky torsos, wristless arms with elbow ball built into the lower arm section, and the kneeball built into the lower leg. The feet here are perfectly straight along the inside arch line. The legs insert into the hip holes in a French manner—more underneath the torso than from the front—and the tops of the old body legs are round like a rake handle top. They are also painted a pale, yellowish white. The buttocks are flat in back without the cheeks common on German bodies.

No. 44 Some Belton-types have a white space between the lips, giving the impression of exposed teeth. This seems to be more common in the later dolls. It is an attractive feature but the dolls believed to be the oldest do not have it.

Of the twenty-five so-called Beltons in one collection, only one has brown eyes which are original. The wigs of these dolls are made of goatskin or lovely yellow mohair.

Bru

Although there are dolls that are rarer, at the moment none seem to have the appeal of a Bru. This popularity appears to be a part of the contemporary trend toward more humanized dolls, which is reflected in the current prices of French as well as German dolls.

What is considered the best among French dolls seems partially to be influenced by the new appreciation of character dolls. Eleanor St. George, in her book *Old Dolls*, published in 1950, stated, "Undoubtedly the French bisque head as made by Jumeau represents the best in doll making." But as interest in humanized dolls with character increased, the demand and popularity of Brus increased. Bru is now more desired than the Jumeau, partly because collectors now realize that fewer Brus were made.

It is wise to remember that the popularity of any doll, including Bru, could be a fad that is subject to change. Collectors should not pay inflated prices simply to follow the crowd.

Coming on the market in the 1860s, the Bru dolls show a certain nonconformity. Many of the Brus have gimmicks designed to appeal to the adult buyer. The second patent by Leon Cashmir Bru was for a two-face Surprise doll. From the patent sketch, one face was sleeping, the other

No. 44

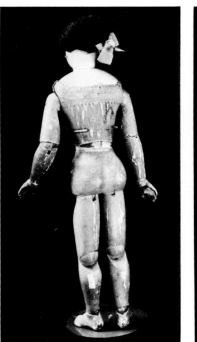

No. 45A   No. 45B   No. 45C

awake. The head could be turned without muss-
ing the hair.

A three-face doll marked **C.B.** was at one
time considered a Surprise Bru. Today much controversy surrounds the origin of this mark.
Perhaps it is German. The initials "C.B." should
not be the deciding factor for purchasing a
three-face doll.

In the early days Brus made French Fashions
with and without trousseaux, some of which
were imported to America.

No. 45 A, B, C A swivel-bisque head Fashion, for instance, was located in a small town in
Kentucky. The wooden body, a minor work of
art, is completely jointed, including the ankles.
The detail in the feet includes the arch and foot
pads; the equally exquisite hands have fingernails. The waist is jointed so that the doll can
bend in all directions. It is not surprising that
Bru claimed that his dolls with carved wooden
bodies had a special grace. On the left side of the
bisque shoulder plate is the rare Bru mark, **B. Jne
cie.** (*Cie* means company.) On the right shoulder
is the mark **F. Depose.**

The face has more character than normally
found in a Fashion. Her profile has a resemblance to the later Bru. The eyes are blue
paperweight. As with the Jumeau Fashions, earlier eyes are not as beautiful as the later ones.

No. 46 A, B The Brus with kid bodies of the
1880s are some of the most desired of the Brus.

The fine bisque head swivels on a bisque shoulder plate with a slightly molded bust. The mouth
is closed with a faint suggestion of tongue or
teeth. The paperweight eyes have feathered
lines. The multi-stroke brows are not as heavy as
on a Jumeau, nor do they touch the bridge of the
nose.

The mark **Bru Jne 7** appears on the head and
shoulder. The stuffed kid body has a childish
shape, readily identified as one made by Bru.
The upper arms are of wood covered with kid.
From the elbow the arms are made of excellent
quality bisque. The curved hands are a
trademark of Bru. The wooden legs are pin-
jointed.

When Chevrot bought the firm in 1883, the
products of Bru apparently had a good reputation. He kept the name "Bru." Chevrot advised
customers to make certain that the Bru dolls bore
the manufacturer's identification. The wording
in the advertisement raises an interesting point.
One would expect a manufacturer to say: "Be
sure your doll is a Bru." Instead, the ad states,
check that "your Bru doll" has the Bru name.
This could mean that competitors considered the
Brus worth imitating. An unmarked doll resembling a Bru should not automatically be
labeled as one.

Chevrot owned the company for eight years,
then sold to Paul Girard, who used some of the
earlier molds. But many of his dolls have a differ-

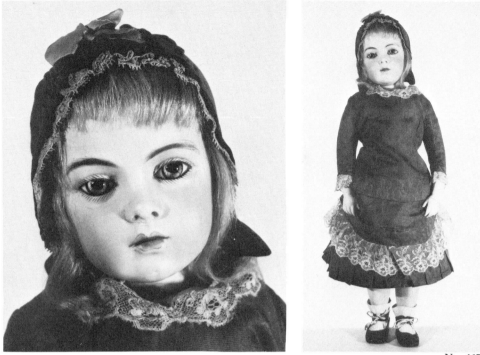

No. 46A

No. 46B

ent look from the older Brus. Collectors think his open-mouth dolls with sleeping eyes do not meet the standards of the earlier dolls. However, because the name is Bru, the prices are high. In 1892, Girard added an **R** to the **Jne** mark.

No. 47 A, B, C, D An all-original sailor lad has the mark **Bru Jne R 7**. His factory costume is made of red faille and has hand embroidery on the sleeves and edge of the breeches. The red featherstitching is more effective on his white nautical collar. The outfit is completely lined, as was customary at that time. The brown leather high-topped shoes with gold buttons are marked on the bottom with an oval **Bru Jne Paris**. His height is 18 inches.

The bisque head has a closed mouth and pierced ears. The paperweight eyes are brown, a color that Bru made more successfully than Jumeau. Although dark, the eye reflects light and shows depth.

Damage does not seem to have as drastic effect on the price of Brus as other dolls. Bru heads which have been shattered in as many as seventeen pieces and completely repainted have been sold. A repainted bisque head usually has a freshly powdered look. If in doubt on the amount of repair, insist on the right to check the inside of

the head, where damage is not as carefully covered.

A Bru body, with a marked German head is not regarded as a rarity or especially valuable. It is simply a Bru body with German head. A rusted neck assembly is not evidence that the head is an original. Producing the rust is not difficult. The application of such a common household product as vinegar will supply impressive rust in a short order. Even if a head was replaced years ago, it is doubtful that parents would pay for, or that a doll hospital in this country could supply, a Bru head in the proper size. Inasmuch as it made no difference to the child, an available head was used. There is evidence that German products were customarily used as replacements for broken heads.

Through the years, when doll hospital proprietors retired or died, their inventories were sold or auctioned. These sales seldom failed to produce old stocks of German heads in many sizes, still in their original boxes. Even the boxes and labels are similar, indicating that the market for separate German heads was so widespread that all box manufacturers were involved. It is seldom that such a box comes to light with the maker's name included on the label. They usu-

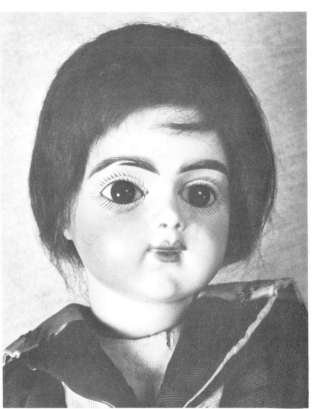

No. 47A

No. 47B

No. 47C

No. 47D

ally say, ''Dollheads'' or ''Dollhead'' and ''Made in Germany.'' An ample space is provided for the factory to stamp its own information as to size, stock number, etc.

The odds against a collector finding the correct head for a Bru body are great. Today dealers and collectors are reluctant to sell a head separately.

No. 48 Although the ''Kissing Bru'' is a late example, the doll is made of excellent quality bisque. The blue dress still has its paper label. On the original box the instructions are printed in English, confirming that the doll was made for export. The label on the box reads:

''BéBé BRU   Kiss BABY
Pat. applied for. Made in France

Raise the right arm up to the shoulder, turn the head towards it, pull the cord, and Baby throws a Kiss.''

One of the myths of the doll world is that after the S.F.B.J. corporation was formed, the Bru dolls and molds were discontinued. This myth has no basis in fact. Not only were these dolls available in France, they were also imported and advertised in this country. Paul Girard was the first man in charge of S.F.B.J. It is not logical that he would ignore his own inventions. As late as 1947 the *Societe Francaise Bébé & Jouets* advertised dolls marked with the name "Bru." The trademark of "Bébé Bru" was renewed in the 1950s by S.F.B.J.

Other French Dolls

Novices sometimes overlook the fact that Bru and Jumeau were not the only French firms to make excellent dolls. A collector should include A.T., Gesland, Steiner, and Rabery & Delphieu if he wishes to consider well-known French dolls.

Dolls with the initials "A.T." are among the loveliest of the French dolls, and rarer than the Brus. A.T. dolls are preferred by some collectors, and generally are more expensive than Brus. However, during a Regional Convention of United Federation of Doll Clubs in 1971, with all attendees voting to select the best dolls in competition, the A.T. lost to a more common French doll. Because the A.T. dolls are so rare, they are not always recognized. The German mark "A.J." is sometimes mistaken for the unusual French "A.T."

No. 49 This **A.T.** has lovely threaded paperweight glass eyes. The white lines radiating from the pupil can be compared to spokes in a wheel. The doll's head is made of excellent bisque, with closed mouth and pierced ears. Her body is the French jointed type. Her wig of old blond mohair is a muted color instead of the garish shade of modern mohair. She is estimated to have been made in the 1880s, but the identity of the manufacturer of the A.T. dolls has not been authenticated.

Another French manufacturer, F. Gesland, was more famous for his padded jointed bodies than for the heads he manufactured. The marks on the heads of F. Gesland dolls often are **Eden Bébé**, **F.G.** and others. The F.G. heads are thought to be made by Ferdinand Gautier. The early F.G. heads have the initials cut in to the bisque at the hair line.

No. 50 A, B A 14-inch doll, whose head is marked **Eden Bébé**, has the Gesland stockinet-covered body with composition shoulder plate,

No. 48

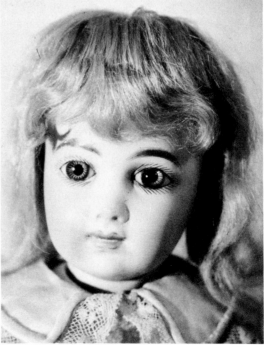

No. 49

arms, and legs. Her swivel head has an open mouth with large round teeth of the German style. Her mouth is so wide open that more of the teeth are exposed than usual, creating an unattractive toothless gap on one side. However, her blue glass eyes are French paperweights of the feathered variety. This type may have been more difficult or expensive to make since it is least common of the paperweights. Her eyes appear to have tiny pieces of ostrich feathers imbedded in the background glass. Being without a strict pattern, feathering permits the color to appear at its true depth and creates a lifelike appearance. Her multi-stroke eybrows are even thicker than those of a Jumeau, although they do not touch the bridge of the nose. The ears are pierced. This rare size doll has stamped on the body—

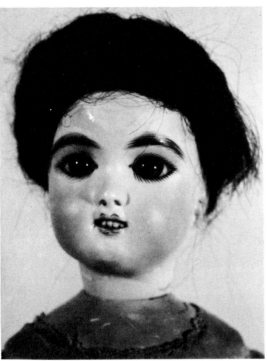

No. 50A

BEBE E. GESLAND
BRE   S.G.D.G.
5 Rue Beranger .5
Paris

Eden Bébé is the trademark of Fleischman & Bloedel. This German firm was one of the founders of the *Societe Francaise de Fabrication de Bébé et Jouets.* Although this company's property was confiscated during World War I, S.F.B.J. continued to use the trademark "Eden Bébé" for many years.

The initials **R.D.** have been used by two contemporary firms, Rabery & Delphieu, and Roullet & Decamps. The latter made mechanical dolls and sometimes used heads made by other firms.

No. 51 The 25-inch mechanical walker has beautiful bisque head resembling a Jumeau, with the mark **P 12** up by the hairline. Back of the right ear is a faint red **H** often found on Jumeau dolls. This head could be a replacement, though R.D. did occasionally use Jumeau heads.

The walker mechanism is a key wind clockworks type with the winder shaft protruding from the right side of the body. The key has the initials **R.D.** on it. When the doll is wound up, the weight of her body takes off the brake and she walks and cries. The brake releases the spinner so that the spring can go into operation. The main portion of the mechanism is attached to the inside back wall of the torso; rods on each side of it extend down and fasten to the inside of the legs.

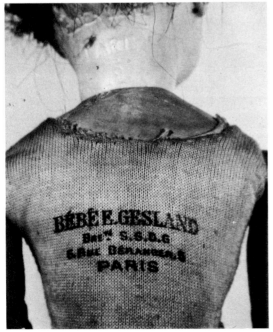

No. 50B

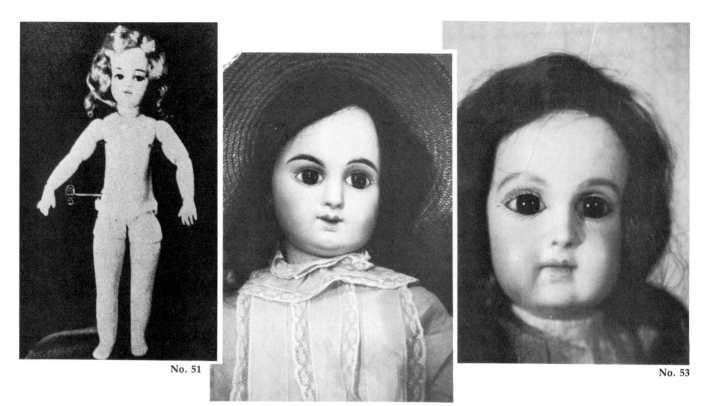

No. 51

No. 52

No. 53

The June 28, 1892, French patent calls for the attachment of the rods to half a ball joint at the top of each leg. In the patent sketches, the inner half of the ball joint is shown cut away, but in the doll itself it is the outer half that has been removed and the attachment made to the inner side of the crotch half of the ball.

In a German version of the "R.D. Walker", the mechanism was simplified to reduce cost by removing the entire ball joint.

The variations between the patents and dolls demonstrate that patent records can not always be regarded as completely accurate.

There are more French doll patents than collectors have been able to straighten out in years of serious, on-the-spot research. It was one thing to secure a French patent; it was something else to have the doll manufactured. Some serious researchers feel that if not one specimen of a doll is unearthed in the years that knowledgeable buyers have been searching in France, then the doll was only patented, not manufactured.

No. 52 Made by Rabery & Delphieu, this doll is typical of the desirable French dolls. Her bisque is good quality with delightful fleshlike coloring. She has a closed mouth, stationary eyes, and pierced ears. Her sturdy French body has a pale yellow finish and unjointed wrists. However, she does have a fairly common flaw; there is a coloring blemish on her cheek. Probably a worker touched her head while the complexion coating was still damp, removing some of the color. This pretty doll is quite a contrast to an open mouth R.D., which seems homely.

More and more the dolls made by Schmitt of Paris are becoming appreciated by collectors as an example of the finest quality of French dolls. In the 1970s Schmitt dolls have won the honored title of Best in Show at several doll conventions over Brus and wooden articulated French fashions.

No. 53 The closed mouth Schmitt doll with pierced ears has stationary eyes and French style of decorating. Her facial expression is more like that of a quiet but alert child than of a doll. The dark-eyed lass resembles a long-face Jumeau. The unmarked versions of this particular Schmitt model are sometimes confused by inexperienced collectors for the Jumeaux. Nowadays, the Schmitt is considered more valuable than the

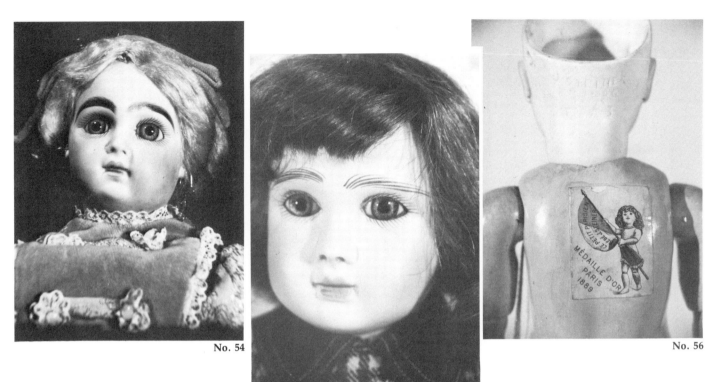

No. 54

No. 55

No. 56

typical closed mouth Jumeau. Unlike some of the Jumeaux, the Schmitt does not have applied ears. The mark on the Schmitt doll is:

The body, which is also marked, has more hip and stomach modeling than most, and flat buttocks, It has huge ball-shaped joints at the hips instead of the legs fitting directly into the torso. More than a dozen firms had names which are quite similar to Schmitt. Even some of the marks are similar but the dolls bear little resemblance to the highly prized French doll.

No. 54 Incised with the mark **W.D.**, this 15-inch doll could be considered French. The pale yellow composition or papier mâché torso has wooden limbs. The wrists are not jointed. A smaller **W.D.** (not pictured) has wooden arms, jointed at the wrist. Both have pierced ears, a closed mouth, and stationary eyes. Only the 15-inch doll has shiny multi-stroke eyebrows. The thick bisque heads have the slightly coarse texture of the earlier French bisques. As in the case of A.T., we still don't know what the initials represent.

No. 55 A 23-inch Steiner has a rather late mark. The words **La Petite Parisian Bebe Steiner** which are found on the left hip of the doll indicate it was made in 1889, the year the trademark was registered, or later. However, the style of the body is of the early French type. On her head is incised:

Steiner
Paris
P. A. 15

The decorating of her head is interesting. Her thin eyebrows are feathered with spaces between the strokes. Pretty blue-gray eyes are surrounded by upper and lower eyelashes. Her closed mouth appears slightly parted. She lacks the usual dark lines outlining the lips. As with many Steiners, her dome is made of cardboard instead of the more expensive cork usually associated with French dolls. Of course, her ears are pierced.

No. 56 This is a close-up of a paper label placed between the shoulders of a 13-inch Steiner. The trademark is an illustration of a doll holding a Steiner banner. The word "doll" is used deliberately. The drawn figure has a ball-

No. 57A

No. 57B

joined body instead of the shape of a real child. The date, 1889, represents the year that the firm won one of its gold medals, not necessarily the year that the doll was manufactured.

No. 57 A, B The children made by F. G. have a special charm. The decorating is typical of the French style including the feathered eyebrows, outlined lips, and delicate lashes. However, this 19-inch doll has her own special look. She has the unjointed wrists and oversized hands associated with the early bisque with composition bodies. Her mark is **F.7G.** No. 57 B shows the large hands and unjointed wrists typical of fine French dolls.

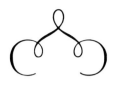

German Dolls
With Bisque Heads

German dolls are often the first that beginning collectors become acquainted with because these dolls are generally more available and cost less than French.

German dolls can provide an excellent opportunity for a developing collector to learn to interpret the significance of doll markings. However, a wise collector will avoid any tendency to become a slave to marks.

While the impulsive novice may completely ignore marks, the collector with only a smattering of knowledge may turn down an excellent doll because its maker had a reputation for ordinary dolls.

Even the presence or absence of the word "Germany" may be interpreted in different ways. In 1891, Congress passed a law that required imported goods to be marked with the country of origin. On a swivel head, lack of the word "Germany" incised in the bisque does not necessarily place it prior to that date.

There was, as always, an interim for compliance, creating a twilight zone for some of the bisque doll heads. It is generally believed that the first dolls to comply with this law were stamped. The odd placement of the word "Germany" on some heads is good evidence that their makers stamped the word to heads already in production; speedy handling through U.S. Customs could mean an important sales advantage. However, no one knows how many thousands of completed dolls warehoused abroad, or in transit, or piled in our retail store stockrooms, escaped stamping. Also, a doller should keep in mind that some firms used stickers that soon washed off.

Nor should a shoulder head marked with the word "Germany" be quickly judged as being made after 1891. There is much evidence supporting the theory that many firms, proud of fine workmanship, particularly in bisque shoulder heads, incised them before the United States' country-of-origin law went into effect.

If "Germany" is hidden under the glued-down kid shoulder piece on a shoulder head, the date is variable; but if it is clearly in sight above the kid edge, then 1891 is the earliest possible date to allow it—most likely it is later.

A doll marked only with the word "Germany" should not be called an unmarked German doll. These are usually newer than the dolls without any marks. Late in the 19th century, and in the early 20th century, the bigger German companies sold and rented their molds to lesser firms. Often no identification was included. This was such a common practice that these products do not have any unusual value although they are an interesting part of the history of the German dolls.

A doll with an odd German mark, in contrast to one with an uncommon French mark, is not necessarily expensive. The workmanship by the more obscure firms was often substandard to the well-known giants of the doll industry. While many collectors enjoy having dolls from a variety of companies, they hesitate to pay a premium price solely because a doll was made by a small business.

Armand Marseille

Dolls made by Armand Marseille (commonly referred to by the initials A.M.) are regarded as the most common. Advanced collectors regard dolls made by A.M. as late since production did not start until the 1890s. Since Armand Marseille at its peak made one thousand heads a week and it continued in business until 1929; it is little wonder A.M. dolls are found in great profusion. What is overlooked is that there are a surprising number of faces and an unbelievable variety of novelty and "character" types, and great range in quality.

Dolls with the incised marks **370, 390,** and "Floradoras" are among the most readily available and at the moment should be among the least expensive.

No. 58 In contrast to the A.M. examples mentioned, this lovely lady doll, 14 inches tall, has some unusual features. Under the wig she is incised:

"Armand Marseille, Germany
401 A 5/0 M"

She could have been made for the French trade. She is very "un-German." The closed prim mouth is an orange color; the corners of her eyes and the nostrils are decorated with dots of the same orange. The painting of the eyelashes around the socket and the multi-stroke eyebrows add to her delicate appearance. The multi-stroke eyebrow means the painting was done with more than one stroke of the brush. The face is an oval shape instead of the usual round. The chin is actually pointed.

The slender body is as interesting as the face. Today many collectors call such a body "flapper" type. The legs are well proportioned with a narrow ankle. The small foot is arched so that she can wear high heels. The thighs are shorter than the average German doll; this keeps the ball joint of her knees from showing when she wears shorter dresses. The wristless arms are jointed at the elbow. The torso is molded to represent an adult woman.

Her clothes are as elaborate as the teen-age fashion dolls of today. The ensemble she wore when originally purchased in the early 1920s is not a factory-made outfit, but was made by a seamstress for the retail outlet. The fur trimmed coat and blouse and skirt are the length of the early, not late, 1920s. Her silk stockings with garters and her pearl necklace are factory originals.

No. 59 A, B, C The **401** lady dolls are good examples of quality variation within the same model. The bisque of one on the left (A) is excellent. The closed mouth example (B) is made of high color painted-on bisque which is susceptible to peeling; the colors used in decorating the

No. 58

features are too vivid to seem natural. Each doll should be judged on an individual basis. Despite being made of painted bisque, C's wardrobe and trunk would make her a charming addition to any collection.

Although never made in quantity, dolls with this adult type of ball-jointed body were made throughout the 1920s. The 1928-29 Montgomery Ward & Co. catalog illustrated a similar doll labeled: "An Exquisite Doll to Dress." This doll has an open mouth with teeth, silk crepe chemise, pearl necklace, silk stockings with garters and "daintiest high heeled slippers." One could conclude from the drawing that this was the same doll, except for the puzzling comment in the ad, "Slender type, exactly like a child."

No. 60 "Mabel" is an ordinary and poorer quality A.M. Her fat cheeks are typically German with a highlight on the nose and a deep dimple in her chin. Her orange pink mouth is open with seven added teeth. Her eyebrows are ridged and painted with a heavy stroke that almost meets at

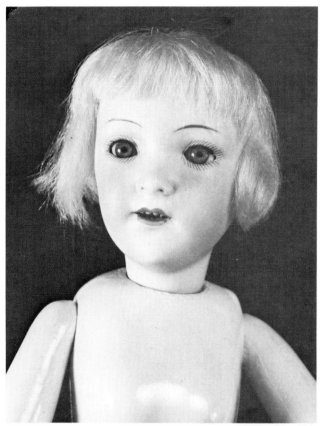

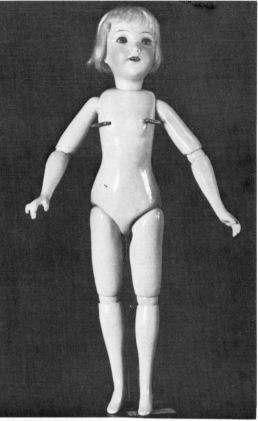

No. 59A

No. 59B

No. 59C

No. 60

on the body instead of having the French style of hooks and eyes. Occasionally, interesting outfits were produced, but unless a dress is spectacular, German dolls are not bought for ensembles. Because the clothing was not particularly attractive, children were usually eager to discard it. "As found" clothing, on the other hand, can be quite nice because mothers, grandmothers, and aunts used to make beautiful doll clothes. Today many well dressed dolls are wearing these presents from loving elders.

No. 61 At first glance this delightful character of 1900 appears to resemble a Gerbruder Heubach. However, the marking on the center back of the head, **Made in Germany A 3 M** leaves no doubt as to her origin. Her blue intaglio eyes have a tiny drop of white bisque applied on the upper lid as a highlight.

The eyelids are well molded; the brows are one stroke in light brown. The entire face is pink without much contrast in the cheeks, and the lips are a pretty orange pink without the darker center line often found in closed mouth dolls.

One of the ironies of doll collecting is that intaglio eyes are now highly prized; in the Butler

the nose, three light strokes above the broad strokes. The dark brown eyes have a flat appearance and the black pupil is visible only on close inspection. Her shoulder head is incised in script **Germany Mabel 7/0** which indicates that she is one of the early A.M. dolls. The wafer or gusset jointed kid leather body is also an early one. The seat wafers are sawdust clogged, which keeps the body too stiff to bend properly. Her clothes should be labelled "as found" since they are not factory made.

The term "original clothing" on German dolls is misleading in that it implies an especially desirable feature. On most German jointed dolls, factory clothing consisted of a flimsy chemise with cheap lace trim and pants of the same kind of material. Often costumes were nailed or sewed

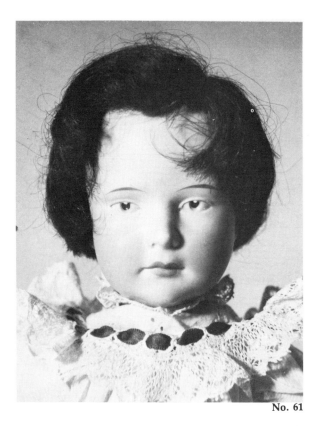

No. 61

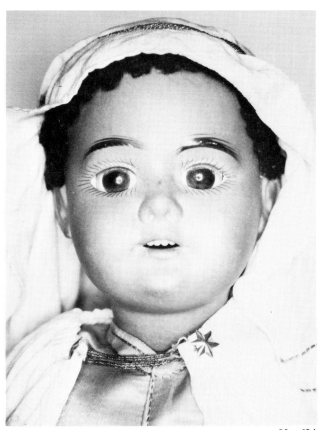

No. 62A

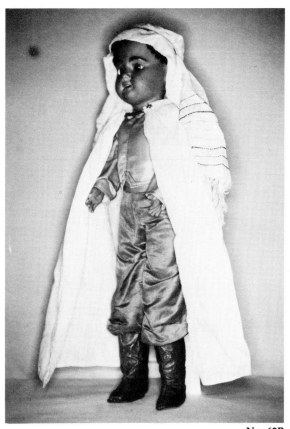

No. 62B

Brothers catalog of 1908, moving glass eyes are stressed as a sign of quality.

As with other enterprising manufacturers, A.M. also made dolls of different ethnic origns—Oriental, Negro, and Indian. At present, German Orientals with molded Oriental features, are in the most demand, Indians in the least.

No. 62 A, B The name "Hindu Boy" is said to have been on this lad's original box. The head is incised in four lines: **1894 A M/DEP/Made in Germany/ 2-1/2.** The dull bisque is tobacco brown; the brown sleep eyes have brown waxed lids, painted eyelashes, and multi-stroke black brows. The open mouth has teeth added after firing and the lips are bright scarlet. The close-curled wig is made of black knitting yarn which was glued right to the head and dome without a gauze cap. The ears are well molded and prominent.

The reddish brown body is fully jointed, the stick leg type, with wooden kneeballs embedded in papier mache-and-plaster lower legs. The

shoulder balls are wood and are part of the wooden upper arms. Fingernails and toenails are not outlined.

His original clothing is detailed and interesting. The head scarf is of fine white cloth, chainstitched in silk at the ends in yellow, red, and blue stripes to form a "Roman" border; edges are fringed. It is held on by a wire halo, covered with gold braid.

The flowing cape is the same white material with a narrow braid loop at the neck. The clothes, which fasten with hooks and eyes, are cotton-backed satin, lined with lightweight buckram. The jacket is deep aqua bordered with chainstitched double rows of yellow silk. The wide, pleated, body-fitting belt is cerise; the "bloomer" pants a vivid Prussian blue. He wears long black stockings and high, dark tan kidette boots with yellow paper soles. He just invites display with a nice hide-covered old fashioned toy horse!

No. 63 A, B One of the early talking dolls was made by A.M. A label on its kid body

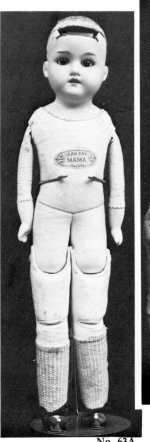

No. 63B

No. 63A

No. 64

exclaims "I can say Mama." The mechanism was operated by a lever in the back of the head.

No. 64 The fact that the trademark for the "Just Me" doll was registered in 1929 probably means the doll was one of the last created by Armand Marseille, and because production by A.M. was drastically reduced in the late 1920s, this is an uncommon doll. It is found in both bisque and painted bisque. This example's head is made of painted bisque that has a yellowish tint, but the cheeks are quite rosy. The untinted bisque beneath her mohair wig could indicate fast or careless production. She has sleeping blue eyes and a close, pursed mouth which is described by collectors as a "rosebud type."

The enameled body has little detail, and is jointed only at the shoulders and hips. The right arm is molded in a bent position while the left is straight. The doll is 10 inches tall. Incised on the head are the marks:

Just Me.
Registered.
Germany
A. 310/7/0. M.

King Kestner

Dolls by Kestner were also popular, and today they are still respected. This firm was making beautiful dolls and heads long before the French got the knack of it.

Many Kestners are available because the firm, established at the beginning of the 19th century—production of bisque material began in the 1860s—was still advertising in **Deutsche Speilwaren-Zeitung** in August, 1929.

No. 65 Even the ordinary Kestner dolls have an appealing quality. This 15-inch girl, marked **154 Dep. 2-1/2** on the head, is a good example. The incised **Made in Germany** on the shoulder covered by the kid body indicates that she may be earlier than 1891. The bisque is desirably pale; the open mouth has molded teeth instead of added glued-on teeth. Kestner was one of the few German firms to copy this French style. The dark blonde eyebrows are multi-stroked. She has sleeping blue eyes surrounded by painted eyelashes with a red dot at the corner of each eye. Still glued on the plaster dome is her original pale blond mohair wig. The wafer-jointed kid body has stuffed feet of cloth; her hands, well molded with good detail of fingernails and wrinkles, are lightly blushed with rose color.

Because of Germany's home industry, the coloring of highlights, lips, cheeks, etc. was done by whole families, including small children. The blushing of hands was probably the assignment for the children who couldn't be trusted with the valuable heads. This system of cheap labor and low overhead allowed the German manufacturers to undercut the prices on French dolls and still make a profit.

No. 66 The next Kestner is decorated in a similar style, but she is more valuable because of her open-closed mouth with two lightly molded teeth. An open-closed mouth is molded open but there is no actual cut through the mouth. Such dolls have a character look; also there are fewer dolls with an open-closed mouth. Her blue eyes are French paperweight. Unless the plaster dome has been tampered with in some unapparent manner, the eyes can be considered original. A deeply incised **6** is at the rim of her cut bisque head. Underneath the scalloped kid body is the

No. 65

No. 66

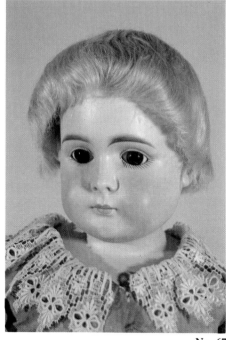

No. 67

mark **B, Made in Germany 6.** There are four sew holes in the shoulder. Because the entire body of the doll is kid, it would have been a more expensive originally than a cloth-bodied doll. She is 18 inches tall.

No. 67 This pensive lass is a transitional doll. Made before the United States country-of-origin law went into effect, she was not marked in the mold, but was stamped **Germany** in red on her shoulder to permit importation. Another Kestner product of quality, the shoulder head has a cloth body and bisque forearms. She is about 24 inches tall. The big glass eyes do not sleep, the mouth is closed, and the wig is mohair.

No. 68 A swivel-head character of the early 1900s, this doll resembles a younger child. The body is a replacement. One wonders if a toddler body would have been correct. She is marked:

Made in
C Germany 7
143

No. 68

The molded roll of fat under the chin is similar to the Kestner babies. Her cheeks are prominent; the nose is broader than usual; and the multi-stroke eyebrows are arched. The two glued teeth instead of the average four makes her even more juvenile. Even though a later doll, the bisque is still of pleasing pale quality.

No. 69 This doll from the 1900s, with the famous **J.D.K.** mark is a googlie or goo-goo eyed character. To dollers the terms ''goo-goo'' and ''googlie'' mean painted or glass eyes which look to the side. The impish faces of goo-goos almost invariably remind outsiders, especially comic strip buffs, of the Katzenjammer Kids.

This doll has sleeping goo-goo eyes of brown. Her mouth is open with two teeth glued in place. The decorating of the bisque is excellent and subdued, with none of the ''high'' coloring associated with late German products. Instead of a squat body made of inexpensive cardboard, she has a toddler body jointed at the elbows, wrists, and knees. Kestner googlies are eagerly sought by collectors.

No. 70 Even though this doll is marked only with numbers it is suspected to be an early bisque Kestner. The shoulder head of pale bisque is lightly turned. The doll has a solid dome with no holes. It was made before the manufacturers

No. 69

No. 70

began the economical practice of making dolls with open heads to lighten shipping weights. The deep chest has shoulder marks and four sew holes. Incised on the shoulder is the mark **639 #6.** Her closed mouth is of the Kestner style, with attractive pink rose color.

The lips have the square ends, which means the mouth was painted with a stenciling mask instead of free hand. This practical Kestner firm, unlike some of the other German manufacturers, did not depend on talented artists for decorating. Anyone could paint the lips by using a stenciling mask.

The body on this doll is a replacement, but this model has been found with both manufactured and homemade cloth bodies. Perhaps the head was rather expensive, and some families saved money by making the bodies. The eyes are usually stationary for this doll.

Inexperienced collectors are sometimes disappointed to learn that such a lovely doll is thought to be German. However, it is considered a choice doll because it is an early one made of excellent bisque and has a closed mouth and stationary eyes. The German origin does not decrease her quality or desirability.

Dolls marked **698** are very similar and are also considered Kestners. The open mouth version of the doll has the mark **698-1/2.**

No. 71 A wide-eyed alert child, 34 inches tall, has several desirable features. She has a closed mouth, stationary eyes, and excellent kid body with the Kestner crown label. Surprisingly, the arms are composition which are attached to a cylinder that runs through the body below the bisque shoulder plate. The clothes and wig are not original.

No. 72 German dolls designed or inspired by Americans are among favorites of collectors. The Kestner Gibson Girl of the 20th century is an excellent creation based on the Dana Gibson. Many firms made dolls resembling the Gibson Girl, but Kestner had a copyright on the words "Gibson Girl."

This delicate adult has an oval face, sleeping eyes, and a slim ladylike neck with a slight indication of a throat hollow. Her carriage is proud with head tilted slightly upward. The mouth is closed. The famous Kestner dome is covered with a mohair pompadour wig. The Gibson Girl bodies, either cloth or well-proportioned pin-

No. 71

No. 72

jointed kid, were not always stamped with the name Gibson Girl. However, lack of the name does not decrease the current value of the dolls. Many still wear the familiar paper crown label of "King Kestner," but the Gibson Girl is royalty without a crown.

Gerbruder Heubach

Gerbruder Heubach, one of the most beloved German doll makers, made characters which appear to be miniature portraits or real children instead of commercial dolls. These dolls, considered superior by many collectors, often convey strong emotions instead of the usual bland expressions found on dolls of other manufacturers.

A collector should be careful not to confuse Heubach of Kopplesdorf with Gerbruder Heubach. Most Heubach of Kopplesdorf products are quite ordinary when compared to Gerbruder Heubach.

No. 73 The molding and decorating in the crying boy is realistic. There are three definite frowning creases in his forehead, with one-stroke

eyebrows slanting to emphasize his wrinkles. The intaglio eyes with large iris are squinted in distress. One eye has an applied bisque highlight. Heubach highlights in the eyes were applied with a brush. The bisque hardened in firing. A molded tongue is the focal point of his wide open-closed mouth. The lips are painted thicker than usual, perhaps for emphasis. One can almost hear his howls of protest. His solid dome head has painted brush strokes to represent hair, another device also used by Kestner. The ears are prominent and deeply molded. His coloring is high as is that of most of the Gerbruder Heubach dolls. This little boy, if on the doll market, would find a home quickly.

For awhile it was assumed that Gerbruder Heubach dolls with intaglio eyes and closed and open-closed mouths were earlier dolls. However, in the A. C. McClurg & Co. General Catalogue, 1915-16, the life-size baby character dolls resembling Heubach are illustrated with painted features; the price was $4.30 for a half dozen.

No. 74 Although her bob with bangs is a late style hairdo, this doll has the so-called earlier intaglio eyes and closed mouth. The dull blond hair is painted without any special attention to individual brush strokes; the eyes have shallow pupils with highlights and gray blue iris rims.

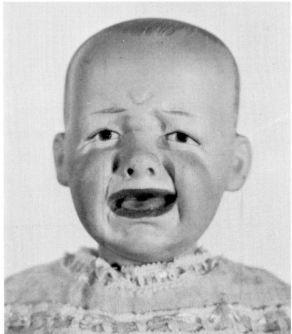

No. 73

The smiling mouth has a dark line separating the lips. The complexion coat is very rosy, another feature associated with late dolls.

With the economical process of pre-coloring _____ inside of the head is the same _____ Frequently, the so-called _____ de with this later method. _____ usion is that Heubach con- _____ make _____ er type heads to beat the competi_____ in _____ rtant item of cost. They had to _____ cheaper b_____ se they eliminated so many e_____ assembly _____ teps, plus the outside cost of eye_____ blinker ba_____ s. They were also lighter in we_____ _____ to pa_____ k, and shipped with less brea_____

No. 74. The _____ ful Heubach also used the same _____ s on figurines and dolls. This happy boy _____ d on both. His hair is molded _____ style. The Heubach children _____ wigs and flocked hair. (In the pr_____ ng, the head is coated with glue, the_____ to a blowing treatment of flocking powde_____ _____ stroke eyebrows are in a natural po_____ intaglio eyes are glanc- ing to the side _____ the highlight dot. His mouth is open with_____ added teeth.

It is amazing _____ hile excellent workman-

No. 75

ship and bisque characterize the Heubach heads, the bodies are poorer than those of vastly inferior competitive dolls.

It would be incorrect to call some of them composition bodies; they are more like compress- ed punk or pulp with plaster added to bind it. Hip-and shoulder-jointed in many instances, are difficult for collectors to restring without a high speed drill because they break under hand- boring pressure and melt if water is used to soft- en the plugs which hold the rubber. The paint was poor quality, generally without a glaze. They attracted dirt like magnets and washed down to the peculiar composition even when care was exercised. The cloth bodies were not models of workmanship either. Made of sized bright pink or white muslin, they are outside-stitched with white or machine overcasting. The hands are some form of composition. The feet are either the same material or crudely formed of cloth.

Purchasing a head in hope of finding a cor- rect body is always a gamble, but with the swivel head of Heubach, the odds are poor. Many man- ufacturers bought their doll bodies from the same source, but the original bodies for Heubach must have been especially made because the necks of Heubach heads are longer and smaller at the base than other German heads of the same period. Seating them in the neck hole of a body from another doll is often impossible, and doz- ens of bodies can be tried before a satisfactory one is found; not right—just satisfactory. With such appealing faces, who looked at bodies!

Sometimes a manufacturer can even be iden-

No. 74

tified by the way the word "Germany" is used. Even though the marks were not always copyrighted, the special marks of dollmakers were not copied.

No. 76 A The odd lettering of **GERMANY** is a Gerbruder Heubach mark. It seems strange that while the German firms respected the trademarks of rival companies, identical dolls are found made by competitors. One explanation is that sometimes the companies took orders from each other.

Heubach did have some trademarks using his name or initials. **No. 76 B** seems to be the traditional mark and the combined **G.H.** initials at the lower half of the die is quite distinct. The top of the design is sometimes referred to as a "half daisy." At times this trademark is found in combination with **No. 76 C.** The Heubach square seems to form an oblong which often is very small. Inasmuch as marks can be very small, a good habit for a collector to acquire is to carry a magnifying glass at all times, and to **use** it.

No. 76 D A fourth mark stamped on some Heubach heads and some figurines is a small circle with **MADE IN GERMANY** between the two rings which form the circle. The circles are either in vivid shades of green or, less often, red.

Nos. 77 and **78** are examples of almost identical heads; only the style of decorating differs. **No. 77** is a Gerbruder Heubach; **No. 78** is an Armand Marseille.

Heubach of Kopplesdorf

Huebach of Kopplesdorf products were made for an inexpensive market and current prices are usually within reach of the collector with limited funds.

Heubach of Kopplesdorf is thought to have been a brother-in-law of Armand Marseille. A great rivalry existed between the two, not in the doll business but in horse racing. The fact that the Heubach firm was not as great a commercial success as Armand Marseille was reflected in their personal competition. In the early 1900s

No. 77

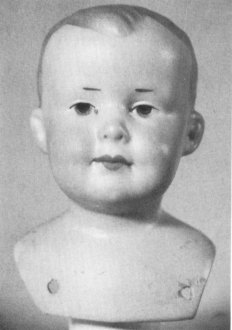

No. 76A

No. 76B   No. 76C   No. 76D

No. 78

Heubach's stable consisted of only four horses, while Marseille owned 30.

No. 79 The 11-inch girl with molded straight hair appears to be a Polynesian. She is made of inexpensive painted bisque of reddish brown color and a toddler body of the same shade. Her stationary eyes are black without any contrast between the pupil and the iris. The molding of upper and lower eyelids creates a character look.

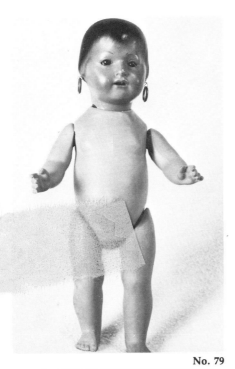

No. 79

No. 80

She has a thin straight nose. Orange dots are found at the corners of the eyes and nostrils; her multi-stroke eyebrows are painted brown with a reddish tint; her open mouth is bright orange with two teeth glued in place. There are deep comb marks in her black painted hair. She has only a slight indication of ears which are covered by her hair; the large brass earrings are pierced into the head.

The incised mark on the back is difficult to read, but appears to be

> Heubach Kopplesdorf
> 452.   15/10

The word **Germany** is placed so low on the neck that it is covered by the composition body. Her head must be bent forward to make it visible. The toddler body is of the inexpensive type, jointed only at hips and shoulders.

No. 80 A 9-inch toddler made by Heubach Kopplesdorf is all original, including the dress, petticoat, gauze pants, socks and shoes. In the mass production, even the hem of the inexpensive dress was sewn by machine. The doll has blue sleeping eyes and a wide open mouth with two upper teeth. The blond mohair wig is straight and bobbed short. As expected, the decorating of the bisque is just adequate. A neck socket was omitted, a characteristic that is common in this type of doll. Incised on the head is the mark

> Heubach—Kopplesdorf
> 300   14/0
> Germany 22

Simon & Halbig

Simon & Halbig, one of the giants of the industry, made millions of dolls with a surprising range in varieties and markings. The quality of the products depended on the market.

France's prestigious Jumeau firm was not above purchasing heads made by this German company for its market of Jumeau bodies. With wigs glued tightly on the bisque heads covering the German marks, the dolls sometimes passed for French. Mistaken identity still occurs. The use of Rabery & Delphieu French patents by Simon & Halbig suggests that Jumeau was not the only French firm which had a commercial connection with S & H.

At the other end of the scale, Simon & Halbig supplied dolls for street vendors. Since these products seem to have been made for at least sixty years, a collector needs more than the origin of the firm to date and judge quality.

No. 81 An early example (probably from the 1870s) of shoulder head with completely molded features is incised **S & H** in script on the lower front ege of the plate. The yellow hair, drawn back from the brow without a part, falls in nicely molded locks at the shoulders in back. A black "Alice" band crosses the center skull to ear top. The ears are pierced through the head. The painted blue eyes are convex; the eyebrows are a single stroke of medium brown; the old red eyeline is very fine; in place of lashes the top lids are lined in black. This style of suggesting lashes was used by S & H as late as the 20th century.

The early sawdust-stuffed body, made of sized cotton instead of the later tough drill, has a

No. 81

No. 82A

No. 82B

center seam back and front which creates a smooth shaped waist at the sides. Drill is a heavy fabric of linen or cotton which has a diagonal weave.

No. 82 A & B This 12-inch lady doll is of such fine quality some might mistakenly label it as French. The fashion-shaped wooden body is covered with drill. The solid dome head has a swivel neck lined with kid. On the shoulder plate are the initials **S & H** in script. The arms have exquisite detailing. The separate thumbs would require additional time in production. She has lovely paperweight eyes with red dots at the inner corner. The bisque, of exceptionally fine texture, has a pale tint. She still has her original braided wig.

No. 83 A, B Another closed mouth doll with a kid lined swivel neck is made of coarser quality bisque. The 15-inch doll has paperweight eyes and heavy multi-stroke eyebrows. The head is

covered with a plaster dome. The sawdust filled body is made of kid all the way to the toes.

No. 84 A, B A doll with a swivel neck and shoulder plate has characteristics which identify it as an early Simon & Halbig. The head has a solid dome and is incised with initials **S H 3** and the number **908**. The shoulder plate has the mark on the front, which is usual for this type of doll. The mouth is closed, but S & H did make an open mouth version. The stationary threaded eyes are in nice proportion to the face. The ears are pierced through the head and the base of the neck is lined with kid, French style. Although made of drill, the sawdust-stuffed body has the center seam. She is 13 inches tall.

Nos. 85, 86 Two ball-jointed dolls with the same markings, **1079**, vary in quality. The word **Germany** on the inferior doll (No. 86) dates her after 1891. Part of the contrast seems due to changes in production. Toward the 20th century,

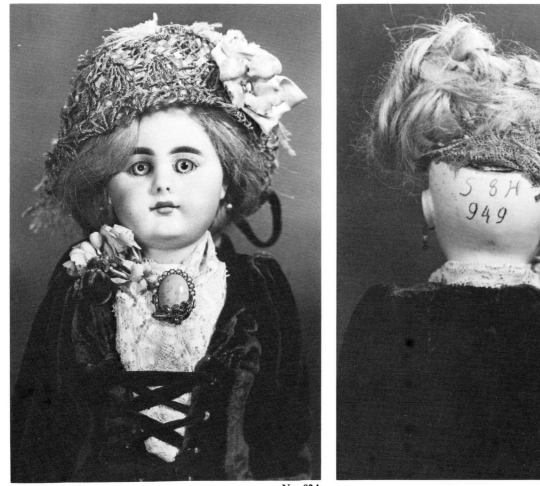

No. 83A   No. 83B

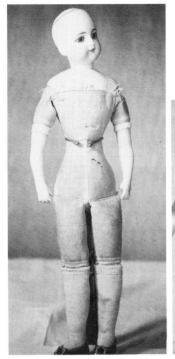

No. 84A   No. 84B

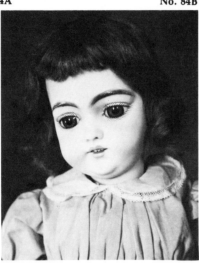

No. 85

No. 86

competition made mass production essential. S & H seems to have allowed less time for the bisque heads to dry in the greenware stage before being fired in the kiln. On the quickly processed dolls such features as full cheeks, nice dimples, and child-like facial quality are lost. The bisque is a pinker tone instead of the paler flesh color. Also, the multi-stroke eyebrows are not as well done. Both dolls have the tie holes to protect sleeping eyes from breakage.

Another **1079,** again lacking the word "Germany," has extra ball joints between the arm socket and upper arms, which adds an attractive width to the shoulder. In 1890 Butler Brothers advertised French Bisque natural jointed or double jointed dolls. In 1908 the style was still popular. That year's issue of **Our Drummer,** the catalog of Butler Brothers, again described dolls with loose ball joints as "French jointed," even while admitting a German origin. In this case, the dolls mentioned were from Kestner, a rival of S & H.

The ethnic dolls made by Simon & Halbig are regarded as prizes because they are less common than the white dolls. They were made from both standard Caucasian molds and from specially designed molds.

No. 87 A, B is a good example of a doll made from a special mold. The baked-on color is pitch black; the sleep-eyes are rather flat and dark brown; the eye wax is also colored very close to black. This is not a "white" doll painted, as many of the brown ones are. The features are African, with a wide nose, short upper lip, and a wide, full mouth. The six teeth are small, like those used by the French.

The mark, **Germany/Simon & Halbig/ S&H / 6,** is mostly covered by the wig cap.

This particular doll is not an early issue. The firm name is written out above the initials used on the old dolls; the word **Germany** appears; and she has the two holes, on either side of the number, through which the eyes are tied. The body is late.

Schoenau & Hoffmeister

Schoenau & Hoffmeister, one of the smaller companies, also used the initials **S & H** with a star; this firm's star had only five points, and the initials **P.B.** are inside it.

No. 88 Truly Oriental in appearance, this girl

made by Schoenau & Hoffmeister shows clearly that the lesser firms did make some unusual dolls. Her black almond-shaped sleeping eyes are molded to slant upwards. Above them are one-stroke brows, painted to suggest a frown. This style of decorating is also found on other ethnic dolls, such as the American Indian. Her face is round with a slight double chin. The color of her body varies slightly from that of her head. Her hands have fingers which are molded together. This style may have appealed to practical parents because the finger survival rate is so good. Her print kimona indicates that she is Japanese or Korean. She resembles a model made by Simon & Halbig. Since the firm Schoenau & Hoffmeister was not established until the 20th century, its dolls are not yet automatically considered antiques.

No. 87A   No. 87B

No. 88

Kammer & Reinhardt

Kammer & Reinhardt claimed to have started the trend in character dolls by marketing a more realistic baby doll in 1910. However, character dolls were advertised in pre-1900 magazines and catalogs, although their numbers in proportion to the more typical of the period were small. In the early doll books the products of this firm were only briefly mentioned, and the legends, although inaccurate, were stressed more than the dolls. Now there is an increasing interest, especially in the character dolls.

In 1927, Kammer & Reinhardt was advertising bisque, celluloid, and wax. Because this is a late date for wax, perhaps the dolls were the wax fingerling candies which were filled with juice with a sweet syrup-like flavor. The wax, which had little taste, was only to be chewed, not swallowed.

No. 89 This gorgeous doll, a full 30 inches tall, is marked **K ✡ R Simon Halbig II.** Some collectors claim they like Kammer & Rhinehart but do not care for Simon & Halbig. Yet Simon & Halbig made many of the desirable characters for **K ✡ R.** The incised star represents the six pointed one of David with "&" in center.

The doll has a closed mouth, blue sleeping eyes, and feathered eyebrows. Her human hair wig is a mahogany color that is associated with people of Irish nationality. Her well-made body is the usual German style with jointed wrists,

No. 89

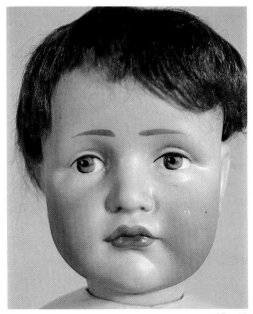

No. 90

No. 91

elbows, and knees. Her bisque's deep coloring appears to glow. The term "greasy bisque" seems inadequate to describe this quality because greasy bisque shines even when dirty.

No. 90 The "pouties" are favorites among the collectors. Incised **K & R 114,** the doll has blue painted eyes and closed mouth. The drooping corners of the mouth emphasize the pouty look; a dark line is painted between the lips; the eyebrows are a bone-stroke almost horizontal line. The upper lid of the molded eye is outlined in black.

The young nephew of Reinhardt was the model for this **114** pouty. In the doll, the shape of the face was broadened. This might have been done to facilitate the use of a two-piece mold. A nine-inch version of the doll has completely jointed body. The body was originally strung with strings from each leg up through holes on each side of the head and tied on the top.

No. 91 Sometimes nicknamed Bellhop, this 18-inch doll is more comical looking and lacks the realism of the other characters. His humorous features include a smiling mouth shaped like a slice of watermelon, a pug nose, brown glass eyes without painted eyelashes, and thick one-stroke eyebrows that appear raised. Also, he has deep dimples and an exaggerated upper lip. On the back of his head is the mark **K & R 124 Simon Halbig.** Eagerly sought, he is truly a rare character doll.

No. 92 Although a marked **K & R,** the doll with its vacant expression and poor quality bisque lacks the appeal of characters. Two glued teeth are placed haphazardly in her open mouth. Even the short human hair wig is not well made. The brown color of bisque is her best feature. She is incised:

Simon & Halbig
K & R
26

No. 92

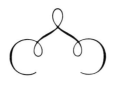

Babies

The saying that everybody loves a baby was not always true with dolls. Near the turn of the century some American families, steeped in Victorian tradition with overtones of Puritanism, had a phobia against using the word "baby". This can be more easily understood when we consider how many children of the late 1800s and early 1900s were reared with a greal deal of help from live-in grandmothers who had strict, even prissy backgrounds; they called legs "limbs" and mentioned babies in whispers.

Naturally, this attitude was reflected in commercial enterprises. In the 71-page Butler Brothers mail order catalog of 1888, which listed everything from accordions to zylonite combs, two pages of dolls were advertised, but there were no dolls resembling babies for sale. There was not a single item listed in the index under the word "baby." However, there were no taboos on illustrations showing women's corsets, and men's apparel. In the 1890 catalog the word "children" is used to describe a knit jacket, intended for babies.

Thirteen years later, the Butler catalog featured only one large baby doll, and that one had a celluloid face. The use of the word "baby" continued to be avoided even when advertising bonnets and carriages for babies. There were only four items in the index under "baby": baskets, cabs, cab robes, and walkers.

Because Americans floundered in the Victorian morass longer than Europeans, it is not surprising that the Old World manufacturers were the pioneers in breaking the bisque "baby" barrier.

No. 93 Simply advertised as "Baby," the Kammer and Reinhardt creation was such a tremendous success that not all orders could be filled. The doll has blue intaglio eyes, one-stroke eyebrows, and a solid dome head with painted brush strokes. The bisque, decorating, and modeling are excellent. The doll even has a baby-like loose muscle on the right side of its mouth, which creates the effect of a drooling infant that is smiling and forgets to swallow. On the back of the eight-inch circumference head are incised the initials:

K & R
100

The copyright was granted in 1909. As usual when a doll is popular, this infant was imitated

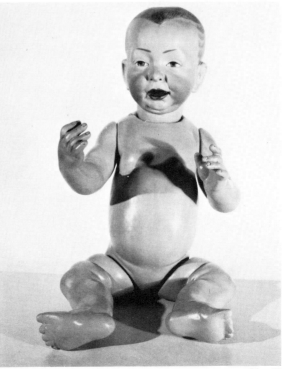

No. 93

by many competitors, including Americans who copied it in composition. A more serious problem for collectors is that German manufacturers reproduced the baby in bisque. The fact that a doll resembles "Baby" does not guarantee that it was made by the respected firm of Kammer & Reinhardt.

No. 94 At first glance this doll appears to be made by K & R, but the only mark on the head is the number **3**. There is a certain softness of the features that comes from making a mold from a production bisque. The painting is noticeably paler, too. The head circumference is 7-½ inches.

A baby doll should be measured by head circumference. Generally, a baby doll sits up approximately the circumference of its head. However, a collector who orders a doll by body length risks getting a head the size of a peanut, because the possibility exists that the head or body might be a replacement. Also, we know from the mail order catalog that there was a considerable market for heads only. Homemade bodies were not necessarily made in correct proportions.

No. 95 The baby was also made in a black version by Kammer & Reinhardt, using the same mold as the original doll. Brush strokes on the head are less delicate than found on most examples of the doll.

No. 96 The Amberg Company once advertised it was the "old house with new ideas." When it came out with the "New Born Babe" in 1914 the idea was about ten years ahead of its time. As with the K & R, the New Born Babe has a solid dome head, but its flattened features create the appearance of a few-days-old baby. It has an alert expression with snappy brown eyes, painted upper and lower eyelashes, closed mouth, and painted muted hair. The cloth body has a squeaker, straight legs, and composition hands. Later the doll was reissued to compete with the Bye-Lo, but the quality of the bisque is not as fine as the originals.

No. 97 Older in appearance than the previous doll, this one made by Kestner is incised with the initials

J.D.K.
Made in
Germany

The decorating of the pale bisque includes upper and lower eyelashes, red dots at the cor-

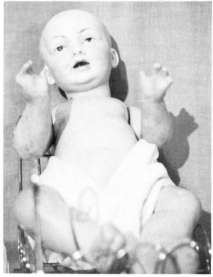

No. 94

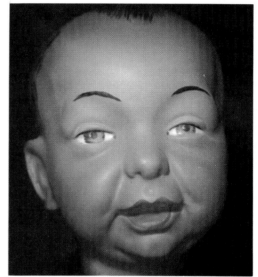

No. 95

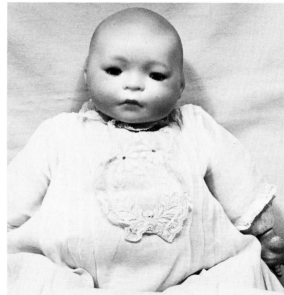

No. 96

ners of the eyes, a slight blush to the cheeks, and multi-stroke eyebrows. The open mouth has molded gum ridges and two lower inset teeth. The brush strokes on the head are painted with careful attention to detail, including swirled strokes at the crown of the head. On a similar doll marked with the Kestner series number **151**, the strokes are just straight lines. This leads to the speculation that the dolls marked with initials **J.D.K.** might have been made for a more expensive market. The ears are well molded and prominent. The brown eyes are not an unusual color for Kestner baby dolls. There is a realistic roll of fat beneath the chin.

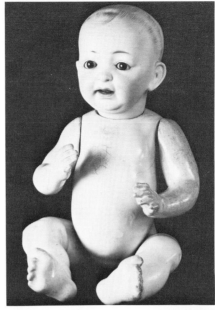
No. 97

No. 98 Among the German Orientals on composition bodies, undoubtedly one of the most desirable is the happy Kestner baby. At the moment, depending on the size, these can be quite expensive. This marked **J.D.K.** is not simply a doll colored yellow. She is just as Oriental as can be and is delightful. The black almond-shaped eyes sleep, the multi-stroke eyebrows slant, and the original human hair wig with bangs is long and straight. Yet there is a family resemblance to other Kestners. The head is 10-½ inches in circumference and incised **J.D.K./ 243.** Many Kestner babies have either toddler or bent leg composition bodies. All the Orientals so far found have the bent leg baby body.
body.
by name in the United States. The incised mark is:

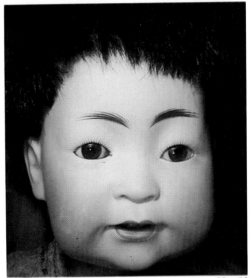
No. 98

Hilda
(c)
J.D.K. Jr. 1914
Ges. gesch. N. 1070
Made in 13. Germany

The blue sleeping eyes are wider, the features of the face are softer, and the cheeks are rosier than in most Kestners. The open mouth with two large upper teeth has a pleasant expression. However, the baby does not appear to be really laughing as described in the copyright. Hilda has a 12-inch circumference solid dome head decorated with pale brush strokes. The doll has a bent leg baby body.

No. 100 Also marked with the name **Hilda,** this doll has a 14-inch circumference head with an open crown, and a blond mohair wig. The expres-

No. 99

sion on the face is identical to the smaller doll. (No. 99). Both styles of Hilda are hard to find, thus establishing it as one of the favorites of collectors. In the South, the 14-inch circumference head Hilda originally sold for around $4.

No. 101 This doll is a good example of an unusual type—an infant with a molded bonnet. The detail of the white bonnet includes molded texture blue lace trim and bows. Blond hair peeks out underneath the bonnet. The rosy coloring of the face is regarded as a late style; above the painted eyes a dark line indicates the upper lid; the open-closed mouth has two upper molded teeth. The composition body with bent legs is an inexpensive variety. On the back of the neck is the incised mark **R.A.** which stands for Recknagel.

No. 102 When looking at this doll made by Gerbruder Heubach, one can easily understand why collectors have nicknamed it "laughing baby." The open, orange-red mouth has a molded tongue and teeth that have a glossy surface. The doll has prominent ears and deep dimples; however, it lacks rolls of baby fat. The high or rosy coloring of the bisque is typical of Heubach. Two tie holes in back protected the

eyes in shipping, and indicate that the doll is late. The bent leg baby body has a pink wash which also suggests it is not one of the earlier babies. Heubach seemed to think small babies were cheap dolls so the smaller bodies were even less well made than the larger ones. Collectors seem not to mind, as long as the bodies stay together. The incised mark is:

All character dolls are becoming expensive, but so many people now collect Heubach that there is rarely a lack of buyers.

No. 103 A little known firm, Davies & Voetsch, produced a baby of excellent quality. Considered rare by some authorities, the doll is sometimes called a portrait type since it resembles a real child. It has light blue stationary eyes, open-closed mouth. On the back of the head is the mark: **D.V**

A similar doll with the same mark has an open crown and mohair wig.

No. 104 A, B This doll is 23 inches tall, has blue sleep eyes and closed mouth. It is one of the few dolls made by Simon & Halbig that does not have the number "9" in the mark. It is incised

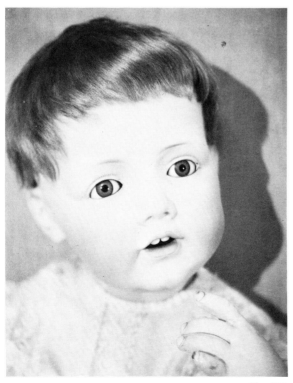

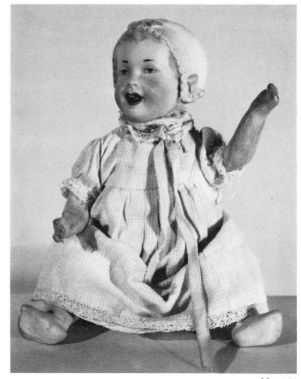

No. 100   No. 101

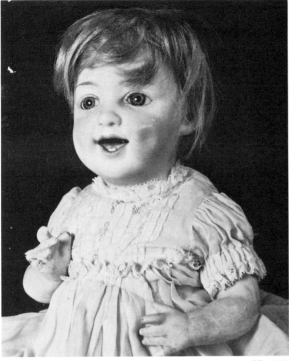

No. 102

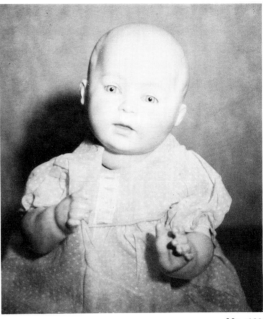

No. 103

1488 and the familiar **SIMON & HALBIG** in large letters is level with the ear lobes. Directly below the lettering, in the center of the neck, there is an oval hole in the head instead of the more common tie holes for the eyes. The head is made of bisque of excellent texture, and has only a comparatively small top piece removed. Like so

many S&H dolls, there are ⅛-inch holes in the bisque close to the cut line. They must have been provided for stringing wires or cords which eliminated the usual neck plug; they are too small to hold the stabilizing bar for a walking mechanism.

The wig is short reddish curls of fur on ani-

No. 104A

No. 104B

mal hide. Although it fits well, it undoubedly is not original because the glue does not match particles attached to the bisque. From the hatch lines on this head glue, one may judge that the original wig must have been the typical German mohair on a gauze backing, unusual to this type.

The hole in the back of the head may indicate that this was made by S&H for someone else. The oval hole measures ¾-inch by ⅜-inch, large enough to carry an incised mark belonging to some other firm. This method has been observed before. A bisque "cookie" of the proper size and shape was incised with the required mark, then kiln fired with a thin bisque rim all around so that it could be glued firmly in place in the hole.

The speculation naturally arises: Was this a stock head belonging to S&H or was it made from molds owned by one or more smaller firms, each of which wanted its own mark fastened in that oval hole? S&H could have reserved the right to market a given number or any that were not paid for within a stated period.

If this doll's body is original, (and that is a big *IF*, even though it is almost mint), it just contributes to the mystery. This particular toddler jointed body with the very short thigh pieces has been found many times on dolls with Heubach-Koppelsdorf heads. However, it is not likely that such an old porcelain manufacturer would have had to turn to S&H for production.

No. 105A, B The Bye-Lo, the most popular infant ever made, was designed by Grace Storey Putnam, who obtained her first copyright in 1922. After World War I, the German manufacturers were steadily being driven out of the American doll market until the bisque Bye-Lo brought temporary new life. In 1925, the Butler Brothers catalog advertised the Bye-Lo baby dressed in a long lace organdy dress with lace trim, or in a pink or blue cotton blanket with white animal figures. The wholesale price of the 13-½ inch long Bye-Lo in the baby dress was $4.50, as compared with $6.25 for the 13-inch Bye-Lo in a blanket. Even though doll buyers were extremely price-conscious then and the dolls were expensive for toys in that era, any quality of Bye-Lo, from excellent to poor, seemed to sell. Which individual firm made a particular Bye-Lo is anybody's guess because, although the artist's name was required on every doll, no identification was usually required of the manufacturer. Anybody who could and would pay the royalty apparently did make them. This accounts for the great variety in the quality of workmanship of the Bye-Los. Not only did the Bye-Lo sell; the dolls

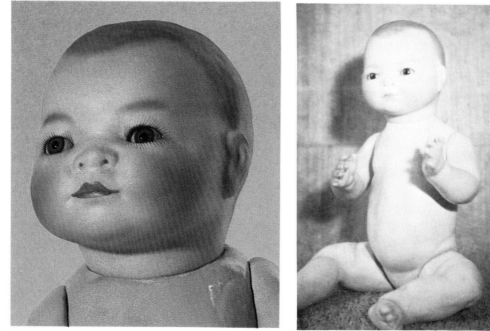

No. 105A   No. 105B

imitating it did, also. The competitors did so well that ads were placed in national magazines advising readers how to recognize a genunine Bye-Lo:

"The genuine Bye-Lo Baby can be easily told from poor imitations by (1) its wonderful life-like face shown here, (2) the name of the sculptor, Grace Storey Putnam, imprinted on the back of the neck, and (3) her signature on the identification tag. They insure your little girl getting the doll she longs for, to love and cuddle." McCall's Magazine, 1926.

This early Bye-Lo with a head circumference of 12 inches has blue sleeping eyes and the hard-to-find composition body. The soft, cuddly cloth body with curved cloth legs and celluloid hands, quickly replaced this more unnatural style. The blue glass eyes are more common than brown. The upper and lower eyelashes are created with black, delicate strokes, a feature that many current reproductions fail to copy accurately. In the original dolls the eyebrows are only faintly suggested, unlike the bold strokes on many copies. It is, of course, possible for a reproduction to duplicate the fine painting of the old one, but reproducers don't usually have the talent or inclination to take that much effort.

No. 106 A very late example of a bisque Bye-Lo demonstrates the risk of collecting painted bisque. Even with the best of care the paint sometimes peels. Even with a touchup the

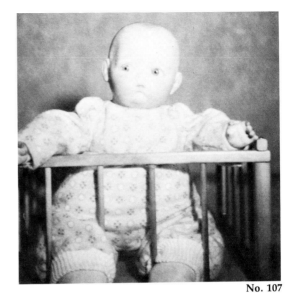

No. 107

effect of the peeling is evident. This Bye-Lo was originally sold as a separate head.

In the 1933 Butler Brothers catalog the only doll of bisque material for sale, excluding the all-bisques, resembled the Bye-Lo. In light of the numbers of Bye-Los produced, the current prices seem way out of proportion when compared to the prices of scarcer, more unusual babies of the same era.

No. 107 The Kestner "Century" baby has a body much like a Bye-Lo cloth body but with

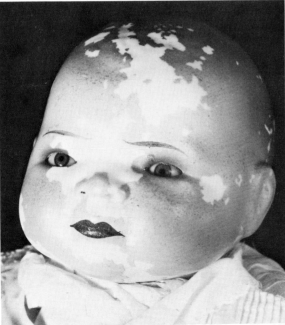

No. 106

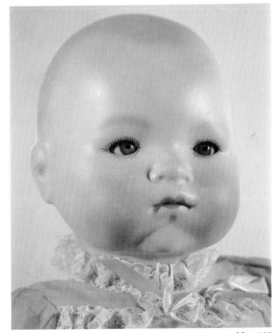

No. 108

rubber hands rather than celluloid. It has sleeping eyes, a closed mouth, brown molded hair, and such a cross expression it makes many collectors want to laugh. The head circumference is nine inches. Obviously competition for the Bye-Lo, it is less common.

No. 108 Armand Marseille made a doll called "Dream Baby," also to compete with the Bye-Lo. It is marked in three lines, down into the rim of the flange neck.

A M
Germany
341/4

It dates about 1924 or 1925; nevertheless, the bisque is beautiful, and the eyebrows barely show. The sleep eyes are blue and the upper and lower lashes are painted. Dream Babies came on cloth bodies, not the fairly good quality muslin used on many Bye-Los but an unbleached cloth of thin, poor quality; it would probably classify as low-count muslin. Nor did Dream Babies have the overlapping legs of the Bye-Lo. The shapeless, stuffed body has straight, center-seamed, sewed-on legs which end in soft fat feet. The sausage-like arms have composition baby hands.

No. 109 This swivel neck infant is marked in four lines:

Germany
G 326B
A.O.M.
D.R.G.M. 250.

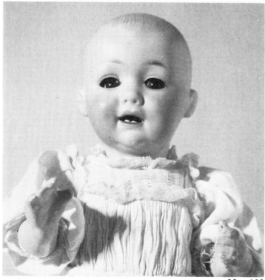

No. 109

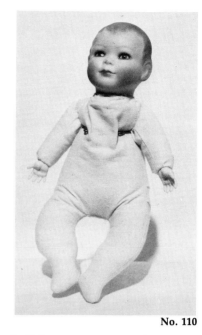

No. 110

Elizabeth Coleman suggests that the **G.B.** indicates Gabriel Benda.

Except for the quality of the bisque, there is nothing about this infant head to indicate A.M. but the pin dot dimple in the chin. The slightly molded hair and the blond brush stroke treatment of the head and the multi-stroke eyebrows strongly suggest Kestner. The coloring is medium and attractive; the sleep eyes are deep dark brown; and the two bottom teeth are doubtless molded in. The bent limb baby body of good quality probably is original, but is unmarked.

Armand Marseille also issued a swivel-neck infant with two lower teeth in an open mouth, (not pictured) incised in three lines:

A.M.
Germany
351/3K

The top lock is more definitely molded in a curl and the hair is sprayed almost orange. It has one-stroke eyebrows, blue sleep eyes, upper and lower painted lashes.

No. 110 The "Fly-Lo Baby," designed by Grace Storey Putnam, is rare. It was copyrighted by the George Borqfeldt Company in 1928. Instead of designing another realistic child, the artist created a magical sprite. The cloth body, so similar to the one used for the Bye-Lo, seems incongruous for a whimsical creature with pointed ears. Although it was made in bisque, painted bisque, and composition, the Fly-Lo was never popular. Due to the rarity of the doll, it is worth considerably more than most Bye-Los. It is incised with its famous creator's name on the back of the head.

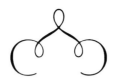

All-Bisque

All-bisques are not the exclusive domain of any one country. Manufacturers and artists in France, Germany, United States, Japan, and China made all-bisque dolls. Because so many of the all-bisques are unmarked, collectors are forced to judge them by their characteristics, such as the eyes—glass or painted—and the types of limbs and torso.

All-bisques are believed to have been made as early as the 1850s in the form of the immobile or frozen Charlotte variety. Today contemporary artists continue to create all-bisques.

Part I French

French all-bisque, which delight and confuse many collectors, are rarely marked, except for the inferior late examples. Being unmarked contributes to the confusion and to unfounded optimism which labels many undeserving dolls as French. The French illustrated in this chapter are classified as early French, for the first type; French type; and so-called dressed French type. In all three categories the dolls have a delicate appearance, are decorated with care, and when dressed have clothes made with exquisite details.

Early French

The early unmarked French dolls are considered to be are finest of all-bisque. Although unmarked, they are identified by the off-set center mold marks. Instead of having mold marks down the sides as the majority of all-bisques do, these dolls have marks on the opposite sides of their fronts and backs, left on one side and right on the other. The French used the off-center design to keep from disturbing the excellent arm and leg sockets when opening the

molds. The hands, large in proportion when compared to other all-bisque examples, often have separate thumbs and molded nails. Sometimes the feet are bare or have four-or five-strap high bootines. The closed mouths are not always molded, allowing the artist great freedom in the way the mouths should be decorated. Sometimes the lips are outlined with a line between the center. The dolls have ball heads and open crowns which often have cork pates, just as in the case of larger French. The bisque with a peaches and cream coloring often has a porous or flaky quality as compared to the sharp and hard feel of German bisque.

These early French dolls are difficult to find and out of the price range of many collectors.

No. 111 The desirable features in this French fashion type includes an original cork dome, swivel neck, glass eyes, feathered brows, and painted upper and lower lashes. The freckling in the bisque helps document this doll as a very early all-bisque. The peg-strung elbow joints are unusual.

No. 112 Unmarked, 4-½ inches tall, peg-strung and swivel-necked, this doll presumably is French because she has more French characteristics than German. The face is oval, entirely without the fat cheeks the Germans loved. The eye sockets are large in proportion: the blue irises are large enough to extend both above and below the eye sockets; and she has both upper and lower lashes. The one-stroke brows almost meet across the nose bridge, as countless French dolls' eyebrows do. The torso has breast modeling; the arms are long; the hands are well formed. The shoulders are flat and closed, and the upper arms are flat on the inner sides. She also has the long, straight, French legs.

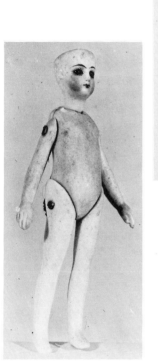

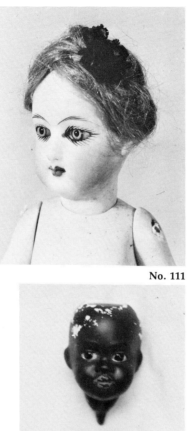

No. 111

No. 112

No. 113

No. 114

French Type

The French type all-bisques also attract collectors' fancies on many counts. Many of the French type have more German characteristics than French, but are superior in quality to German all-bisque. The expression "French type" describes the quality, not the origin, of the dolls. Their faces are sweet and bright looking, and the bodies are generally in better proportion than the average German doll. Another attractive feature is the care with which they were assembled. The little swivel necks often fit into kid-lined neck holes and, on many types, kid disks are glued to the flat surfaces of the arms or legs where they touch the bodies so that they can be moved without making the typical shrieking bisque sound.

Swivel-neck all-bisques are the most desirable of the French type, but novices generally are taken by the tiny set glass eyes, even in the stiff necks. Advanced collectors look for swivel necks, especially those with built-in stringing loops at the bases of the closed necks.

No. 113 is an example of the molded French loop common to French type all-bisques. These neck loops required more expensive molds and better finishing than the other types of loop and are easily identified because they always look like the tops of steeple bells. Besides giving the head more flexibility, the loops and the holes make removing the wig unnecessary when restringing.

German-type swivel-necked dolls without wooden neck plugs often have holes in the sides of the necks to accommodate the arm rubber which also holds the heads in place. The problem with this arrangement is that such heads will not hold a turned position, but will always face front like stiff necks.

No. 114 Unmarked, 5-¾ inches tall, with a plug, this doll is an extreme example of long hair usage. The sleep eyes are threadless cobalt with pupils and only lower painted lashes. Her one-stroke brows are dark blond. The excellent complexion is not pale but it is even and slightly pink.

The body and limbs have side mold lines. The arms are not alike. The legs are sturdy and childish, and the little pale blue, one-strap slippers have molded front bows, barely indicated heels, and yellow soles.

No. 115A

No. 115B

She is quite likely "all original" because the material in her dress is repeated in her tam, and the narrow ribbons in her hair and on her hat are smaller versions of the kind used for her sash. Her undies are sewn on. Her pale blond human hair wig touches the floor behind her.

Dressed French Type (So-Called)

The so-called French type has puzzled many collectors with its combination of French and German characteristics. The German traits include arms that are alike, vertically ribbed socks with blue bands, and a swivel neck with a base hole instead of the molded French stringing loop. Yet in many ways they look French—they have long, straight, slender legs, faces which are less round than the "pretty" German idea of childhood, and typical French decorating styles with painted upper and lower eyelashes and brows that almost touch at the bridge of the nose.

Many of the so-called French-type swivels are peg-strung and, while some have painted eyes, most of them have well-painted lashes and glass eyes, both set and sleep. In the smaller sizes the eyes are usually set and are more often blue than brown, without pupils. As the sizes increase, the pupils appear.

They have legs that are another collector's

joy, primarily because of the great variety. Much daintier than the German-made legs, many of the French legs are barefooted: others have textured stockings in color with vertical or circular molded ribbing. The shoes are also varied in type and color, and include pointed bootines and high button shoes.

These can be found in several sizes under 6 inches, in both swivel and stiff necks. The swivel heads are generally of the pegged variety. The stiff necks are thought to be a less expensive contemporary type. While they are wire strung, they appear to have the same kind of decorating, and are equally well dressed.

These dolls usually command higher prices when found with original clothing. As a general rule the machine-stitched clothing appears to be factory-made because sewing machines are involved in what is obviously professional workmanship. The material is always good and appropriate, whether it is cotton, wool, mercerized cotton, or bright colored felt. The dolls have a chic air about them, which an amateur seamstress could not achieve, even when they are in simple attire.

No. 115A, B For years collectors have debated the origin of these dolls because none of them have been found incised with country of origin. This couple, dressed as Roman peasants, are still tied in their original red box lined with paper lace. The label on the box reveals that the dolls were made and dressed in Germany. On the factory-printed label are the words **No. 99 B-⅛ ⅛ Dts. Tracht**. *Tracht* is the German word for costume. *Roma*, written by hand, is the German adjective for Roman. In the future, evidence may be found that France also made this type doll.

The dolls have brown glass eyes and stationary necks which appear the same as the swivel-neck examples until closely examined. They have the eyebrows which almost meet at the nose and the upper and lower eyelashes which are more common on the swivel-neck. Although the dolls are wire-strung instead of having the more expensive peg stringing, the clothes and decorating are of the same good quality as the swivel-neck dolls. The boy's suit, made of felt, is elaborate, with a green jacket, brown pants, and red velvet suspenders decorated with tiny gold beads that have a molded design. He also has a white bow at the neck, a black felt hat, and curly mohair wig. The girl, her original long brown pigtails covered with a white headdress, wears a white blouse decorated with a blue peasant belt, and a white apron decorated with ribbons and embroidery. The red cotton skirt has contrast of yellow ribbon; around her shoulder is draped a pink shawl; her underwear consists of stiff cotton with coarse lace trim.

No. 116 At first glance, this swivel-neck doll could be considered the same quality French-type doll. On closer inspection the doll has brown painted (instead of glass) eyes with pupil and black line below the eye. The one-stroke eyebrows do not meet at the nose. She does have a pegged-jointed body, arms, and legs with white ribbed socks with blue bands, and pointed shoes with heels and molded straps on shoes. Heels involved more manufacturing steps than the heel-less shoes. The soles of the shoes are a tannish red. Incised on the head are the numbers **298** over **20**. Incised on the legs are the numbers **31** over **8/0** and on the arms, the numeral **4**. The limbs are peg-jointed and the head is jointed by a closed hole in the base of the neck. The now scanty but still curly mohair wig has a machine-stitched part. The muslin cap appears to be original. The doll has a repair at the top of the torso and on the hands.

Part II German

German all-bisques generally seem plentiful and moderately priced when compared with French examples. The amazing variety among German all-bisque adds to the pleasure of collecting. Frozen Charlottes, thick shell bisques, swivel-necks, molded clothes and hair, infants, Palmer Cox Brownies, Kewpies, candystore bisques, pre-colored bisques, flappers, moving heads, comic characters, and dolls made in occupied Germany—all are discussed here to illustrate the imaginative scope and varying quality of the German all-bisque. These dolls were made over a long period of time, from the 1850s to the era of occupied Germany after World War II. It is impossible to describe any common characteristics of German all-bisque with the exception of origin of country.

Frozen Charlotte

The frozen Charlotte or immobile dolls are found in a variety of materials, including china, metal, rubber, as well as bisque. These dolls were made from the 1850s into the 1930s. Some examples are exquisite works of art, but many were crude examples designed to be used as inexpensive party favors in the 1920s and 1930s.

No. 117 A, B, C Incised **Patent Germany** on the back, this frozen Charlotte can serve as a doll, as a bank, or both. In the back of the doll is a slit for depositing coins, but no opening for getting the money out. This feature probably helped decrease the numbers of these dolls that are now in existence. The doll has blond molded hair with

No. 116

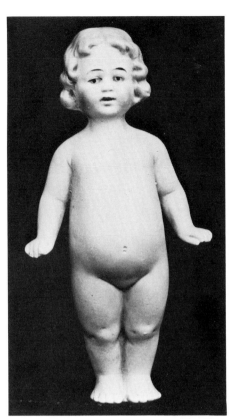

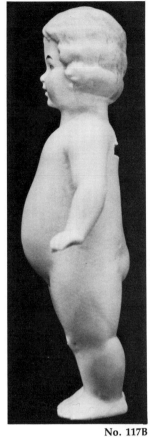

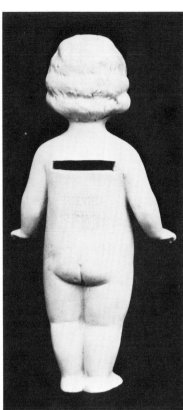

No. 117A   No. 117B   No. 117C

curls falling on the round German face. The blue eyes with pupils have a black lid above each. The chunky body, decorated a pale pink, has well defined hands and feet with individual toenails.

No. 118 AB An untinted white bisque sack, decorated with a molded ribbon, contains three tiny dolls encased in pillows. Dolls wrapped in pillows were popular in the 1870s. The ¾-inch dolls are joined by string which is tied through a hole at the top of each pillow. The only traces of decoration that remain are the black eyes and the pink, green, and blue ribbons of the pillows. Variations of these immobile dolls have continued to be produced in modern Europe.

No. 119 Only 3-⅛ inches tall, this Frozen Charlotte has excellent decorating and detail. Her white costume has molded folds and a belt painted blue. The bonnet has matching blue bows which are also molded. The light blond hair has excellent comb marks.

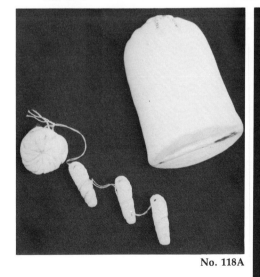

No. 118A

No. 118B

Thick Shell Bisque

The thick shell bisque dolls were not made for the quality market but have an advantage over thin shell bisques in that they are more durable and easy to find.

No. 120 Jointed only at the arm, this 3-⅞-inch very heavy bisque doll appears to be made of almost solid bisque. The doll has a slender

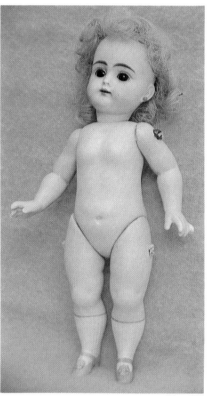

No. 119   No. 120   No. 121

torso, blue molded ribbed socks, and crudely
shaped chunky shoes. The decorating on the face
is not especially good but the solid head does
have its original curly mohair wig. Moths were
so fond of mohair that collectors feel lucky to find
solid bisque heads with an original wig. Incised
on the back are the numbers **273**.

Swivel Necks

The swivel-neck Germans are more expensive than many other examples of German all-
bisque, and the larger ones are much sought after.

No. 121 A lass with sleeping brown eyes has
excellent molding, from her pierced ears to the
rosettes on her shoes. She has heavy multi-stroke
eyebrows and painted upper lashes. This 9-½-
inch peg-strung doll is marked only by the
number **153** on her back. The doll has a closed
neck with string holes on each side in contrast to
the molded button loop of the French style.

No. 122 A 7-inch example is marked with the
S.H. initials of the prominent firm, Simon &
Halbig. Blue sleeping eyes are surrounded by

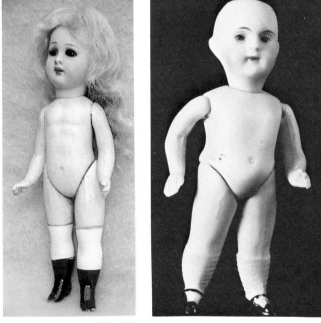

No. 122   No. 123

real lashes. She has an open mouth with a faint
suggestion of teeth. Her long white socks cover
part of her thighs and are a desirable feature. The

loop method of stringing indicates she is a later doll than No. 121.

No. 123 This German doll with a kid-lined swivel neck has bright blue painted eyes that have a large pupil and a white highlight. The orang red mouth has upturned lips, creating the effect of a cheerful smile. There are tiny red dots at the nostrils. She is incised on the head **40 over 0-½**, on the torso **40 over 0-½**, and on the arm **5004**.

The chunky torso has a curved back, round stomach, and a deep navel. The pink socks are ribbed, but do not have a contrasting band. The black shoes have a molded strap, buckles, toe decoration, and tan soles. The doll is 5 inches tall.

Molded Clothes or Bonnets

German dolls with molded clothes as well as molded hair have an almost universal appeal which extends to people who are not collectors. Many of these are made of rather sharp bisque, but some types were allowed to set to only a very thin shell, giving them a hollow sound when handled. The quality in many of them would have been better if they had been more carefully finished, but they were mass produced and, for what they are, they make a valuable contribution to a collection.

Believed to be among the oldest of this type are those with daintily ruffled one-piece underwear trimmed in either pink or blue. Few of these are incised with country of origin unless they are later issues of a previously popular doll. Those that are marked, however, prove the contention that they are German.

No. 124 Incised **6** on the torso and all the limbs, the large 6-¾ inch specimen is strung with old brass wire. The hair is pale blond with fairly good comb marks; the complexion is pale. The brows are glossy brown and the eyes, with centered pupils, have black lid linings and red lid lines; the trim is blue. With the exception of the arms, the finishing and decorating are both well done. The shoulders are closed and the tops of the arms are flat.

No. 125 Negro dolls with molded clothes are not common. The 9-inch doll wears a white suit decorated with blue stripes and a gold belt. The color stands out from the suit. His feet are

No. 124

molded with more attention to detail than his hands.

No. 126 This bonnet appears reminiscent of a Gainsborough-type painting. She wears a large flowing blue hat accented with a yellow feather.

No. 125

Her molded yellow necklace and pink shoes add even more color to the seven inch doll. As in the case of molded clothes dolls, the arms are wire strung.

No. 127 Incised **Germany**, this boy and girl with their animals are later products. The girl wears a molded orchid dress with green collar, matching green bow, and yellow shoes. Bows became popular on all-bisques in the 1920s. A white space is left between the lips to represent teeth. A string around the black cat's neck is attached through a hole in the girl's arm. The boy is dressed in a red, white and blue suit, with a bright red hat and tie. The original gray elephant is attached the same way as the cat. Both dolls are 3-¼ inches tall.

Infants

Many collectors have fond memories of all-bisque infants. These dolls still have avid fans today. Perhaps because of their popularity, the prices of the German infants tend to be higher than those for other German all-bisques.

No. 128 All-bisque babies in tubs were the only infant dolls listed in the 1908 Butler Brothers catalog. These all-bisque babies which could be removed from the tubs must have been good sellers. Seventeen years later in the 1925 Butler Brothers catalog bisque babies in tubs were still featured. One baby per tub was also sold in Butler Brothers catalogs.

No. 129 The largest of the all-bisques pictured in this section, this doll has a head circumference 9-⅛ inches; is 9-⅝ inches high when sitting; 9⅝ inches when lying flat, 14 inches to the heels. It is hip and shoulder-jointed with rubber. The molded glossy yellow hair is beautifully comb-marked out of a center crown and the ears are unusually fine. The painted eyes are brown with high-painted pupils and small highlight dots; the one-stroke brows are brown. There are black lid linings, red eyelid lines, and red eye dots, and nostril dots.

No. 127

No. 126

No. 128

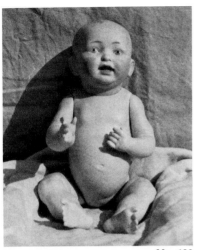

No. 129

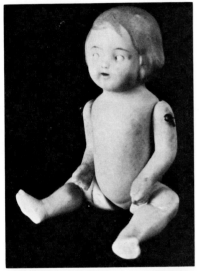

No. 130

No. 131

The entire body is evenly complexioned in a pale tint. The pretty mouth is coral pink with a deeper color center line and has the flat Kestner outer corners. All of the modeling is good and quite detailed in the hands and feet, including fingernails, toenails, and raised big toes.

This is the doll sometimes identified by professionals as "the 13-mold infant." Careful inspection enables one to count the sections, even though it is beautifully finished. All of this elaborate engineering was necessary because of undercutting, which is a recurring problem in molding. Any protruding part, such as the ears, or any indentation, such as the arm sockets, would be broken off in unmolding the soft greenware under ordinary mold construction. Incised on the neck are the initials **J.D.K.,** a trademark of Kestner.

No. 130 This round-face baby has the Dutch boy type molded hair style which is also found on some of the character bisque and composition dolls. The doll has one-stroke eyebrows, red dots at the nostrils, and a smiling mouth. Unfortunately, the paint on the eyes has been scraped off to create the appearance of eyes that look to the side. The torso is incised but the numbers are not legible. The wire jointed arms could be used for all child dolls as well as babies but the chunky legs with wrinkles of fat are only appropriate for babies. The legs are incised **9367-2/0.**

No. 131 Grace Storey Putnam copyrighted her Bye-Lo Baby in April 1922, and these 4-inch stiff-necked all-bisque Bye-Los with painted eyes and hip and shoulder joints were illustrated and advertised in Butler Brothers December, 1925 catalog at $2.50 a dozen. There is a surprising amount of variety in the all bisque Bye-Los. Desirable features include diapers, slippers, and open crowns covered with mohair wigs.

This 8-inch long Bye-Lo has brown sleeping eyes and a swivel neck. There are painted upper and lower black eyelashes with very faint brown brows to match the color of the hair. Incised on the torso is **Copr. by Grace S. Putnam Germany.**

Palmer Cox Brownies

The Brownies, created by artist-author Palmer Cox in sketch and story,—they first appeared in *St. Nicholas* in the 1880s—were a combination of gnomes and elves. The six hard-to-

No. 132

No. 133

No. 134

No. 135

find Brownie dolls shown here, all beautifully molded of the finest bisque, are unmarked but unquestionably German. The trim appears to be the 14-karat gold used on fine china; the colors are bright pastels; and the decorating is expertly done. They vary from 7-½ to 8 inches overall. Each stands on a gold-flecked flagstone platform 2-½ by 1-½ inches, about ½ inch high. The Indian has pitch black hair and brown eyes; all the rest have blue eyes and gray-blond hair.

As in all quality figurines, these little fellows are as perfectly detailed and decorated in back as they are in front. The paints are exactly the same shades in every one, proof that at least six were made as a set.

No. 132 Uncle Sam has a blue-banded white topper with brush marks in the texture to indicate fur felt, a blue swallowtail coat and a white vest with gold bands, a rose bow tie, rose-striped white pants and black shoes.

No. 133 The Bellhop's uniform consists of a rose cap with gold-striped band, gold topknot and chin-strap; a pink jacket with rose collar and gold buttons, a gold trimmed black belt, blue pants with gold banding, white socks and black slippers.

No. 134 The Indian wears yellow feathers, rose and blue tipped, with gold flecking; a blue-belted yellow suit with rose and gold fringe, the molded jacket decoration outlined in gold; yellow leggings with rose and gold fringe, a brown handled gold hatchet; and rose moccasins.

No. 135 The Dude is said to be one of the most popular characters. He is dressed in a blue tailcoat with a gold band, a pink rose in his lapel, a blue-banded white topper with gold edge; white shirt, yellow bow tie; a white vest, gold banded and buttoned, yellow lapels; yellow-handled brown cane; yellow gloves; pale blue gold-banded trousers; white spats and black shoes.

No. 136 The Chinaman has a yellow-banded rose cap with gold knob and trim, a blue smock with gold braid closures, a gold-banded collar, cuffs, and edge, a white undersmock, blue gold-banded pants, white socks, and yellow "Dutch wooden" shows.

No. 137 The London Bobbie's uniform consists of a blue helmet, gold knob, emblem, and banding; a blue coat with a black belt, gold buttons, and all-around banding; a yellow nightstick with gold bands; blue trousers with gold bands; and turned-up black shoes.

Kewpies

Because Rowena Godding Ruggles' delightful book *The One Rose* is so packed with information and pictures by the accomplished American artist Rose O'Neill, her Kewpies among them, it has become a standard reference work for collectors and students.

Patented in 1913, the Kewpie dolls and Kewpie-decorated chinaware, as well as all kinds of novelties, appeared in the 1914 wholesale catalogs. It is said that within the next few years scarcely a home in this country was without a Kewpie in one form or another.

No. 138 The Kewpie couple are all original with the exception of the bride's veil. She wears a crepe paper skirt and carries felt flowers. The groom is a plain Kewpie with his clothers simply painted on him. His hat and flower are of felt.

No. 139 To collectors, action Kewpies are those doing something other than just standing there smiling. This sitting Kewpie holds a now old-fashioned black pen almost as big as he is. The point appears to have been dipped in dark ink, but the white base is blank, as if the Kewpie hasn't begun to write. The Kewpie has the familiar sandy topknot and tuffs of hair, molded eyebrows, black eyes and, of course, the blue wings. Even though the hands grip the pen, the fingers have the definite starfish design.

No. 140 A,B The Traveler with his brown bag and black umbrella is one of the more common action examples.

No. 141 Molded in a sitting position, the Kewpie still has a round paper label with the words **Design Patent**. On the bottom of the Kewpie there is the copyright symbol, **C** incised in a circle. The applied cat has a tan flocked coat. Sitting-down Kewpies came with a variety of animals.

No. 142 In the middle 1950s an advertisement in *Spinning Wheel* announced the reissue of the bisque Kewpies by the Cameo Company. Collectors use the word "reissue" when the original molds are used. This 8-inch reissue Kewpie is made of uncolored bisque that feels scratchy when touched. The overall complexion coating is a darker pink than the older examples and has a

No. 136

No. 137

No. 138

No. 139

No. 140A   No. 140B   No. 141

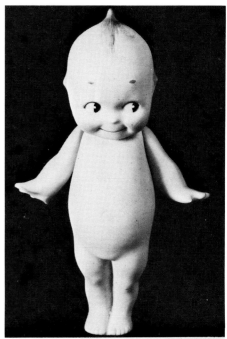

No. 142

grayish cast from the impurities. Other differences in the decorating include gray eyelashes instead of black, and painted highlights in the eyes instead of highlights molded in relief. Incised at the base of the spine is the word **Germany**. Novices should note that the famous Rose O'Neill signature is incised on the soles of the feet. The reissues do not have the value of the earlier dolls, but are interesting inasmuch as they are probably the last authentic bisque Kewpies.

No. 143 This 5-inch novelty doll may have been intended for competition with Rose O'Neill's money-making creations. His eyes to the side, smile and chubby body are similar to the Kewpies. He even has the remnants of a heart sticker on his tummy. He is holding a prayer book with a gold cross.

Candystore Dolls

Most of the German all-bisques in the small sizes are roughly classified as "Candystore Dolls" by many collectors. The commonest of all types, they are frequently incised and almost always have molded shoes and socks. They came to this country by the millions, in an amazingly wide variety. The dolls have mohair wigs or molded hair, often with decoration, and come with either closed or open mouths. Many have more of a character look than the earlier all-

bisques. Price governed the type, the quality, the stringing, and the size.

They received the name "Candystore" because, prior to World War I, boxes of these popular German imports were almost always in the same cases that held the licorice shoe-strings, the chocolate-covered caramels, the sugar babies in pink, white, and brown (they resembled small

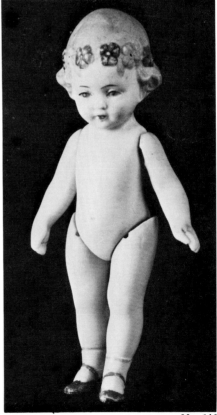

No. 143   No. 144   No. 145

Frozen Charlottes or penny dolls), and the lollypops in rainbow hues.

No. 144 This doll probably was an early attempt to put teeth in all-bisque. The effect was not too successful—the dolls look as if they had buck teeth. The expert decorating includes feathered brows, upper and lower eyelashes, red dots at the corners of the eyes, and cheeks brushed with a soft rose. The brown shoes with two molded straps are decorated with black bows and heels.

No. 145 Only 3 inches tall, this Negro girl has lots of personality. She still wears her original clothing and earrings. Her shiny black hair has good comb marks.

Pre-Colored Bisque

Pre-coloring of bisque for doll heads and parts was an economy measure. The complicated process of tinting could be eliminated by adding pink color to the bisque. From the dolls examined, it would appear that many firms made both uncolored and pre-colored bisque dolls at the same time.

The nicest pre-colored bisque has a dull finish, so pale that it is often difficult to distinguish at a glance because the rest of the decorating is fired.

Another dull finish type is much pinker and less appealing and much of it is post-war. It

No. 146

could have been simply a matter of adding too much color or of substitution due to shortages caused by the war.

A third kind of pre-coloring has a high, unattractive gloss and, since much of the decorating was not fired, the color washes and wears off because it could not get a purchase on the surface.

When there is any doubt about pre-coloring, there is nothing to do but remove the wig to examine the inside of the head. If it is closed construction, the arm and leg flanges will also be pink, whereas those with complexioning are white and have loops that were left white. There is no mistaking the stark white of uncolored bisque. Even the slightest chipping helps also to identify precolored and uncolored bisque.

No. 146 This pale pre-colored bisque has six flowers of blue, red, and yellow in her hair. The flowers and the band circling the back of the head are molded, not just painted. The colors were not fired on and wash off easily. The faded blue eyes may be the result of a face washing. The black eyelid has not faded. The lips of the open-closed mouth are bright red with an uncolored space between. She has uncolored socks with blue bands and brown one-strap shoes with tiny heels. The word **Germany** is incised on the back in script.

No. 147 A pre-colored example, probably from the 1920s, this doll is wire-jointed only at the arms. Her stationary legs and bare feet are molded in a sitting position. One hand holds a small apple. Her sandy colored hair with a curl in the forehead has a hole in the top of her head for a ribbon bow. Her gauze-type cotton dress of orchid appears to have been factory made. On the back she is incised **771 over 8 Germany.**

No. 148 A boy also holding an apple illustrates how the German manufacturers created variations of a similar idea.

Flappers

The all-bisque flappers never had the elaborate promotion that was given to many dolls of the 1930s, so they are a surprise to many collectors. Because they are unexpected, collectors are sometimes misled about their origin. Flappers are sometimes sold as French, although they are actually German. The dolls are slight breasted, slim waisted, and long legged.

No. 149 This 5-inch flapper girl is dressed in

No. 147

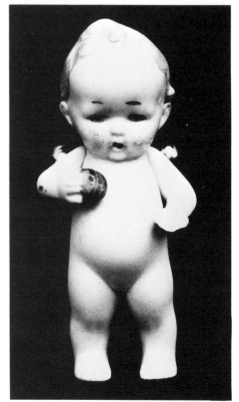

No. 148

No. 149

No. 150

her original factory clothing, which appears in mint condition. The brown felt coat is decorated with a collar made of a pile fabric representing fur; brown paper buttons are glued to the coat. The accessories include a matching felt hat glued on the molded blond hair, and a purse made of shiny red fabric sewed to the coat arm. The hem of the orange cotton skirt is formed by simple pressing, another sign that economy shortcuts were used in production. Though labor-saving methods were used in costuming, the turned head is nicely finished. The blue eyes have pupils; the cheeks are brushed with a dusty orange; the lips are painted brighter orange than the color used on earlier dolls; and the hair has a molded side part, curls, and a few comb marks.

The boy has the same long legs; his reddish brown shoes have molded strap and heels. The wire-strung arms are identical to those of his companion. The head is not turned but the blond hair has excellent comb marks and molded side part. The style of decorating the face is similar to the girl's. Glued to his blue felt coat are lapels, pockets, and black paper buttons. He wears a white shirt and pink tie. As in the case of the girl, the body is marked with the words **Germany** incised vertically on the spine.

Comic Characters

Comic characters have been manufactured in a variety of materials, but collectors are especially fond of the all-bisque examples.

No. 150 The artist's original comic strip character Andy Gump was evolved from a sketch of a real person who had developed osteomylitis, a bone infection, of the lower jaw. The profile of the doll is a perfect illustration of the condition of his chin following radical surgery. The 4-inch Andy Gump doll wears a pale yellow hat, white shirt, orange tie, double-breasted blue overcoat, yellow trousers, and black shoes with white spats. The paint which has been oven-dried instead of fired is peeling and fading. The name **Andy Gump** is incised between the shoulders, and the word **Germany** is incised above the edge of the molded overcoat.

No. 151 "Snowflake" is a cartoon character, copyrighted by Oscar Hitt. The doll's most unusual features are his eyes, which have domes

No. 151

made of isinglass with loose black beads that roll when the doll is moved even slightly. His bright red mouth is shaped like an "O." The molded clothes are made of undecorated white bisque. Incised across the back of his molded pants are the word **Germany** and the name **Oscar Hitt.**

Moving Heads

Although late examples of all-bisque, the moving head dolls with molded clothing are interesting to collect. Often they are called "nodders," inappropriately since the heads move but do not nod.

No. 152 A, B, C Two face dolls of many materials became popular in the 1920s. This moving head doll has one white face and one black face. The only decorating on the pre-colored white face is on the lips of the open-closed mouth and on the black eyes. The paint on this doll was not fired, so even though there are no traces of paint on the hair, it is possible that coloring may have been washed completely away. No part of the black side is left undecorated. The closed mouth

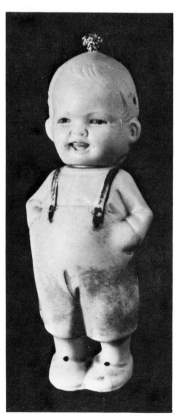

No. 152A

No. 152B

No. 152C

is red; the eyes are white with tiny pupils; the curly hair is the same dark brown as the face. The body is made of white untinted bisque and the shirt is left unpainted. The suspenders are bright red, the trousers, gray blue. The socks and shoes are white, with the exception of the tiny green dots. **Germany** is incised across the seat of the pants. The doll is 3 ¾ inches tall.

No. 153 This pair with moving heads could also be classified as advertising dolls. Still in the original box, the girl wears a red dress trimmed with a gold belt. The boy has a blue jacket which makes a bright contrast with the red cap and pants. The girl has an oval tag printed with the words **Peters Weatherbird Shoes Buy for Girls Germany**. The substitution of the word **Boys** is the only difference in the two tags.

No. 154 In the book *All-Bisque and Half-Bisque Dolls*, a similar biscoloid girl was shown without her mate. Since that time a couple has been located. Biscoloid is a compound which feels and sounds like a combination of bisque and plastic.

Occupied Germany

All-bisque dolls made during the time of U.S. occupation in Germany are usually of poor quality and are more collectible for their historical value than any desirable feature.

No. 155 A, B A late example with an unap-

No. 154

pealing and unnatural orange coloring is loop-jointed and strung with rubber bands. Only the blue eyes with pupils and black lid are painted with care. The cheeks are too orange and the open mouth is bright red. The top of the molded hair is painted a burnt orange while the rest of the hair is tinted the same color as the body. Incised at the base of the neck are the numbers 3502. **Germany** is incised in a vertical line on the torso. Such an inferior doll is interesting because of the words printed on the blue paper label: **Germany U.S.S.R. Occupied**.

Part III Japanese

Many collectors are not interested in any dolls marked "Made in Japan," or even with the older mark "Nippon." Dolls marked Nippon usually are not only considered earlier but of finer quality than those marked with the word Japan. Anyone seriously collecting old dolls should study both varieties of Japanese examples. The Japanese so carefully copied the popular German varieties that it is not always easy to judge the origin of the all-bisques. Sometimes the only evidence that a doll is Japanese is the word Japan stamped on the back, and this can be washed off easily.

No. 156 The dolls of the Morimura Brothers are sometimes considered a notch above other

No. 153

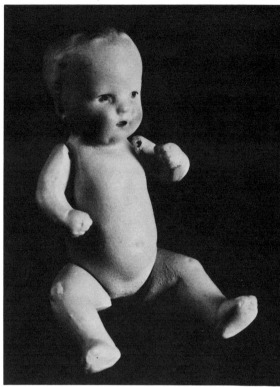

No. 155A

No. 155B

No. 156

Japanese imports. Its "Queue San Baby" came in kneeling and standing positions, with at least two styles of molded caps in a variety of colors. This 3-¾ inch-example has a cap shaped something like a powder blue football helmet with trim of a glossy lavender. He is shoulder-jointed with loops and his half-closed eyes have molded lids with black lid lining and only painted pupils. He has starfish-shaped hands, a glossy black queue down his back, and is made of a very smooth golden yellow bisque with cinnamon specks. He still wears the diamond-shaped label printed with the words **Queue San Baby**.

Morimura produced a sister to Queue San which also came in standing and kneeling versions. The most difficult to find examples of the boy and girl were jointed at the hips as well as the arms.

No. 157 Incised **Nippon**, this 4-½-inch character type doll has wire-jointed arms and stationary torso and legs. The doll is designed to stand unsupported. Her stance is an imitation of some of the German examples. She has molded black curly hair and brown eyes which look to the side. The coloring of the doll is an off-black.

No. 157

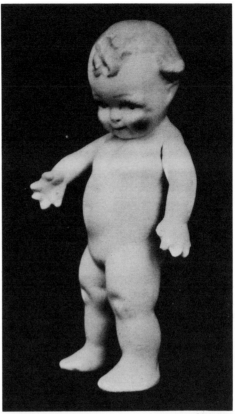

No. 158

No. 159

The only clothing is a pleated straw skirt, Polynesian style, and an orange paper lei.

No. 158 This is an example of how closely the Japanese pirated the German products. If the doll were not stamped **Japan** in red on the back, he could be easily mistaken for the German-made Scootles. He has the same starfish-shaped hands, turned head with blond molded curly hair, and impish watermelon mouth. The body has many dimples and rolls of fat like the German doll. In the decorating there are some small differences. Both dolls have brown eyes, but the 4-1/2-inch Japanese doll lacks the white highlight and black pupils. The yellow hair is a garish Japanese version.

No. 159 This girl's molded costume is a one-piece romper suit with buttons on the front and ruffled collar around the neck. Light orchid in color, the costume is incised on the back **Made in Japan**. The original loop-jointed arms are slightly pinker, but have ruffled cuffs to match the collar. In typical Japanese decorating style, the eyes have large black pupils in contrast to little blue irises. The cheeks are left uncolored, avoiding extra expense and time. The shoes are black with the soles left undecorated.

No. 160 Unlike Scootles, a copy of the German Bye-Lo can be easily identified by the incised words **Made in Japan** which cannot be removed on the back of the torso. The decoration also differs. In the Japanese version the eyebrows are a heavy red orange; the slightly slanted eyes have the large pupils with blue irises painted in a haphazard manner, with parts of the pupil not even touching the iris. Through carelessness, only one nostril has a red dot. The cheeks are orange red; the off-center mouth is dark red. The molding of the hair, instead of creating the effect of curls, looks as if there are dents in the head. From the top of the head to the bottom of the torso, the doll is 6 inches long.

No. 161 A, B Dolls with molded clothes seem to have been a favorite theme with Japanese manufacturers. A 3½ inch marked **Nippon** example has excellent details in molding. If the painting of facial features had been less haphazard she would be quite appealing.

No. 161A

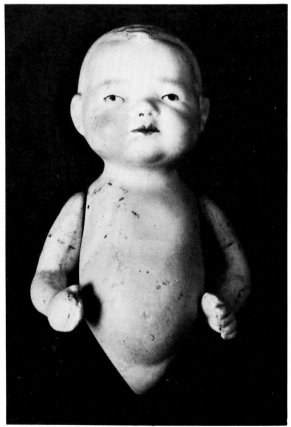

No. 160

No. 161B

Part IV Chinese

The Chinese dolls resemble the Japanese dolls and are usually in the same inexpensive price range.

No. 162 Made of white bisque, this 3 ¾-inch boy with a bald head was made in China. His orange silk tunic, now almost in shreds, is fashioned after the clothing of the northern part of Old China. However, his black eyes do not have an Oriental slant. The brows are a light brown. The nose is broad and flat; the mouth is bright orange; and the round face has a hint of a double chin. Loop-jointed, the straight legs seem out of proportion to the rest of the body. The red painted shoes have a molded strap. The socks are untinted with the exception of the red bands. Incised between the shoulder blades is the Chinese mark:

The Japanese copied the Chinese examples. In the Japanese version the faces are decorated with less care and the double chin has been lost in taking a mold from the original doll.
Another example is identical except for size and a painted black skull cap. The Chinese also used the same head and torso for a baby. The legs were changed to fat, bent limbs with the feet turned outward; the bald head was covered with a brown straight baby wig. The baby is 3 ¾-inches tall.

Part V American

Few early all-bisques were made in America. The Fulper Company did make all-bisque in the 1918 to 1929 period, but these examples are extremely rare and almost impossible to acquire. In contrast, the "Story Book Dolls" created by Nancy Abbott are still familiar sights in second-hand stores. This company, Nancy Ann Story Book Dolls, made painted bisque in the 1930s to the middle 1940s. Contemporary artists are making both reproductions and original creations; the original dolls are more attractive to the serious collector. The new ones are often made in limited editions and are easily distinguished from the German and French dolls.

No. 163 This tiny girl, only 2 ⅝-inches tall, is the only all-bisque member of a dollhouse family called the Prim family, created by California artist Joyce Stafford. Jointed at the shoulders and

No. 162

No. 163

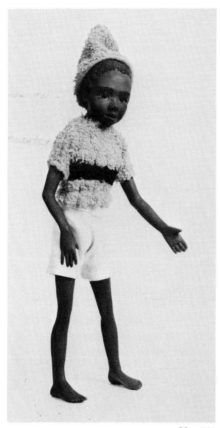

No. 164

hips, she has large painted blue eyes, short blond wig, and bright red shoes. She wears a green cotton dress with matching hair ribbon and sash. The Prim family dolls are accompanied by a certificate showing date of purchase and artist's name.

No. 164 Frankie, an 8-inch lad, has black molded hair, set glass eyes, full lips that are slightly parted. His arms and legs seem long and thin, resembling a child who is growing rapidly. He wears a green stocking hat, shaggy pink sweater, and white shorts. His bare feet are made with realistic detail. A tag with Judith Condon's trademark and the name and issue number of the doll is pinned to his shorts. Judith Condon resides in Florida.

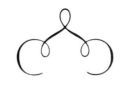

All-China

Just as the phrase "all-bisque" denotes dolls that are made entirely of bisque, the term "all-china" applies to dolls that are entirely glazed. We know from comparing specimens that dolls from the same molds were finished in both bisque and china. We are also sure, from comparing these samples, that this was done during the same time period. There have been suggestions that all-bisques were later products than the chinas, but serious students do not accept this theory.

The all-china designation includes both the thin-shelled specimens which really should be subclassified as porcelain, and the more common thick-shelled and solid varieties. Ceramists call the time required for the plaster of Paris molds to absorb the liquid the "setting up" period. The thickening of the form close to the molds can be watched through the pouring hole by which the slip enters the mold and from which the excess slip is poured off. The excess is drained off through the same pouring hole when the form has attained the desired thickness or has "set up." The length of the setting time before the excess slip, or liquid clay, is poured from the molds determines the thickness of the shell, and the shell determines the quality of the object be it a doll, or anything else.

In quality factories whose products apparently entered the wealthy market in their own day, very frail shells were one mark of excellence. Surprisingly, despite these efforts at quality, some factories did not seem to think highly enough of these novelties to mark them. Exquisite decorating, often including fine brush marks around the forehead hair line, was another quality feature.

German factories, when seeking cheaper markets, either made solid, remarkably durable dolls by not pouring off any slip, or they poured off only a portion of slip and left a doll with a thick, sturdy form. Many such dolls were carelessly decorated with crooked mouths and lopsided or missing eyes under uneven eyebrows. Although such dolls deserve no special subclassification in a collector's personal record, they do comprise the bulk of the specimens available today. They are quite collectible because they represent a period in doll production.

Frozen Charlottes

The now widely used term "Frozen Charlotte" for immobile all-china dolls doesn't seem to have been recognized by manufacturers or distributors. It seems unlikely that European manufacturers would label their products with a name linked to a grim American ballad written by William Carter in 1833 about a girl who froze to death because she refused to wear outer clothing on the way to a dance.

In the 1895 Butler Brothers mail order catalog, these dolls are called "solid china dolls," and were advertised as "penny, 5-cent and 10-cent sellers." In later catalogs, Butler Brothers referred to the 1-inch size as "cake babies."

Evidently solid china dolls were such volume sellers that there was little need to increase the prices to make a profit during the years. In 1895, the 1-¼-inch "nigger penny dolls" sold for 85¢ per gross. More than 20 years later, in 1916, the Butler catalog was advertising a 1-inch black glazed doll for 95¢ per gross.

Collectors generally seem to express more interest in the construction of these dolls than in their original labels or prices. For example, un-

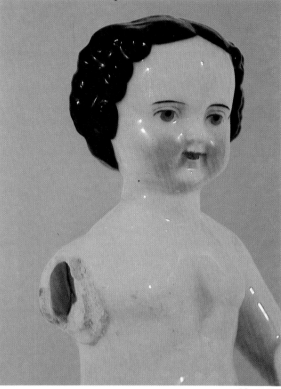

No. 165A

No. 166

less the arms are molded to the sides, all or part of the arms had to be applied or attached after the doll came out of the mold. In some the complete arm was applied at the shoulder, in others the original mold contained stumps of arms somewhat short of the elbow and the forearms only were applied at the cutoff. This accounts for the occasional twisted arms or differences in the position of the hands. No matter how good the workmanship, the application seams can almost always be found because there seems to have been no compulsion to make any secret of it.

No. 165 A, This broken china example illustrates the unglazed, roughened undersurface of the shoulder area inside the remains of the upper arm. This roughness is undoubtedly the drippings from the slip used to attach the arm to the rather large shoulder.

Collectors also ask about the round holes of varying sizes found in the seats of some of these dolls. Collectors sometimes call these "Dresden-type" or "pouring" holes, apparently to make it clear that the word "hole" does not mean that the doll is at all damaged or broken.

Professional ceramists tell us that gases form within these closed bodies while they are firing and the holes permit these gases to escape. They further suggest it is likely that all Frozen Charlottes had such holes but that some firms may have closed them with a plug of clay before the decorating process. Such plugs fired satisfactorily along with the decorating, and that is why we cannot detect them now. Ceramists also say that the holes could have been in other parts of the body, such as the shoulder area. At any rate, a good Frozen Charlotte is neither more nor less valuable because it does not have a visible gas hole.

No. 166 A boyish look is created by the short hair sytle with desirable brush strokes in this 2-½-inch example. The decorating on the face is not as excellent as on the hair. Underneath uneven eyebrows are blue eyes which lack pupils but have a fine black line above the iris. The mouth is the orange color of the old chinas, and the cheeks are pink. The crude body includes a pot belly and short German-style legs with thick calves. In this small size the proportions are not unbecoming. The tiny hands and feet have little detail. There is a roughness on the back of the head, perhaps where a pour hole was filled in.

The doll wears an "as found" costume made of ribbon which has not been removed.

No. 167 Perhaps this is a brother to the previous doll because the bodies are so similar, but the decorating of the face is far superior in this example. The eyes have pupils and red lines above them. The brush strokes are all across the head, not just at the sides. The lines are so fine that the paint on the brush must have been almost dry when used.

No. 168 A, B All chinas were often advertised with the true statement that the dolls would float. This one looks as if she might be ready for a swim. The colors used on the doll are unusual; decorating includes a green head band, pink belt, and light yellow garment. The folds in the garment, feet and hands are well defined. There are red lines above the eyes, a style used on the older chinas. Generally Frozen Charlottes with molded clothes are older than the Candystore all-bisque with molded costumes.

No. 169 This doll has a white molded bonnet with a red ribbon under her chin. She has red lines over her blue eyes and her cheeks have a slight pink blush. The molded fists do not have as much detail as the feet. The left leg is slightly forward as though the doll might be taking a step.

No. 170 As in the case of china heads, an all-china with blond hair is not as common as

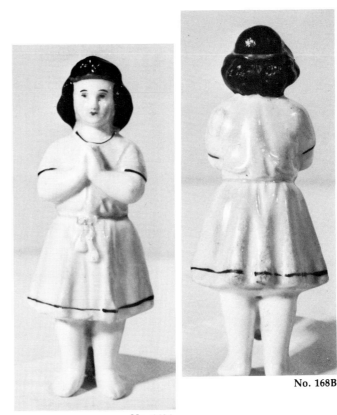

No. 168A   No. 168B

No. 169

No. 167

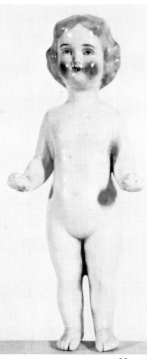

No. 170

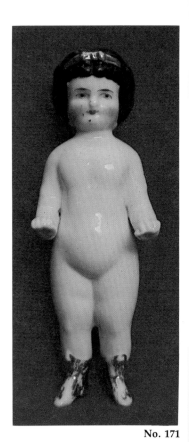

No. 171

No. 172

one with black hair. This molded blond hair is parted in the center with curls on either side. The body is more slender than in many Charlottes. The big toe is separated from the other toes.

No. 171 The gold luster bow enhances the value of this example.

No. 172 Boyish looking, this doll has at least Two desirable features: the 11-½-inch height, and the painted brush strokes. He has red lines above his eyes, painted pupils, and very rosy cheeks. His body is quite thick and he is heavy to lift.

No. 173 The majority of all chinas were made quickly and lack artistic decorating. The 1-inch example is a kind often used as party favors. The arms are safely molded on the chest, making it unnecessary to use the time-consuming procedure of applying arms.

No. 174 This example fits the category of a doll because it could be played with. The baby, swaddled in a blanket, rests its head on a red pillow and holds a rattle. The blanket is aqua blue, the bows are purple, and the colors of painted designs are orange and gold.

Jointed Chinas

Jointed chinas deserve the appellation "rare" because, in contrast to Frozen Charlottes, collectors can spend a lifetime inspecting and buying dolls without ever seeing one of the hip- and shoulder-jointed types. A shoulder-jointed specimen is also a great prize.

Although jointed chinas are regarded as the most valuable, they are certainly not among the

No. 173

No. 174

oldest. The solid pillow dolls were marketed from the 1850s, but in the 1908 Butler Brothers catalog the only white glazed all-china advertised was jointed. Two inches tall, it sold for the wholesale price of $1.40 a gross. Another jointed example, which was illustrated with molded hair, was listed as "out."

The current scarcity of the jointed chinas may be due in part to their original price. An unglazed jointed china (bisque) 2-¼ inches tall, was advertised for only $1.15 a gross. With the cut-throat competition in the doll market, a 25-cent difference in gross price was considerable, because children, who were often the purchasers of the small dolls, guarded their pennies.

No. 175 The rarest of the all-chinas is one that is jointed at both shoulders and hips. The black hair has a flat top style. There are red lines over the eyes and the cheeks are quite rosy. The body has realistic molding including a navel. The

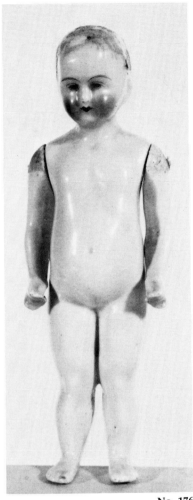

No. 176

No. 175

legs are short and chunky with rolls of fat. In contrast, the arms seem longer and more slender. The hands are clinched in fists.

No. 176 Another unusual example is jointed only at the shoulder. The head which is bent slightly forward originally had a wig. The doll has red lines above the eyes and has brows, which are brown instead of black. The detail molding includes ears, a throat hollow, and individual fingers. The stomach is pronounced, but the limbs are more slender than in **No. 175.**

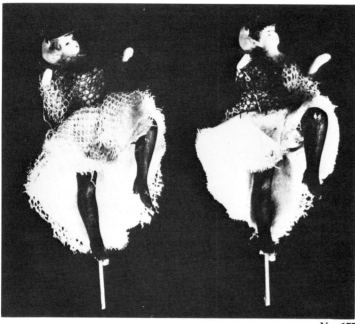

No. 177

No. 178

No. 177 Less than 2 inches tall, these Can-Can girls are jointed at one knee. When the wire extending from the stationary foot is pushed up and down, the jointed leg twirls.

No. 178 All-chinas must have been popular, or Japan would have never entered the market. This brown-eyed Betty Boop is incised **Japan** on her back. Even though she was made in the Orient, the doll is now a rare specimen.

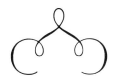

Parian

Parian, one of the classifications of bisque, is a smooth texture pure white porcelain. In Parian dolls only the features such as hair, eyes, lips, and cheeks are decorated.

No. 179 A, B Both china and Parian dolls with this hair style are called Dagmar, supposedly after a Russian countess of the 19th century. There are tight curls on the head with wing-shaped curls at the temples; in back are two buns and two braids. The blue enamel eyes have the unusual feature of upper and lower lashes. A molded bodice has painted gold buttons.

Incised on the front shoulder are the numbers **884.** This could be a clue to identifying the manufacturer. Scratched on the back shoulder is the number **3,** which is probably a worker's mark to identify the one who painted the doll. Workers were often paid by the number of pieces they finished, so a mark such as this does not add much to information about a doll.

No. 180 This light brown-haired beauty has glazed trim on her shoulder and in her hair. Most American collectors would use the term "china trim" to describe this feature. The white glazed trim ruffle on the shoulders is decorated with blue dots and gold borders. There is a gold trim border on either side of the ruffle on the shoulder plate and an applied pink flower with green lines at the neckline. The decorations were applied in the greenware stage, the first step after being removed from the mold. The term "greenware"

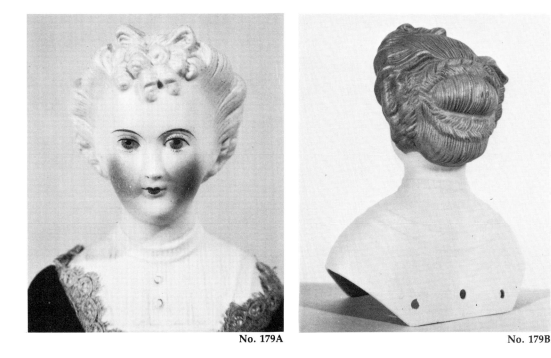

No. 179A   No. 179B

does not come form the grayish green putty color of the pieces, but the fact that objects are unfired and hence unusable, like green fruit. Most of the Parian decorations are applied; the elaborate decorations would have created too many undercuts for molds to have been practical. It is not surprising that many dolls with the same hairdo have different trim. Part of the ruffle on this example has been broken, a misfortune often found on Parians since the applied decorations are fragile. The hair style is not especially elaborate, but the brush strokes and black luster band with a pink bow create an aura of elegance. This example is minus a body. Even though many Parians were originally sold as heads only, a doll with a new body should now be classed as incomplete.

No. 181 Not all Parians are elaborate. The flat-top hair style used for chinas were also used in Parians. Collectors generally prefer the more elaborate Parians, the ones without extra decorations can seem rather plain.

The flat-top style yellow hairdo has a center part, raised temple wave, and curl-covered ears, with comb marks of excellent quality. Irregular vertical curls in back create a bob effect. She has dark blue painted eyes with red lines above, yellow eyebrows, and an upturned mouth. There are four large sew holes, instead of the usual two or three.

No. 182 We describe this Parian as having a squash hairdo, inasmuch as the blond curls are squashed across the front. There is a center part in the crown with comb marks from the crown to behind the back of ears. She has a molded band which is placed horizontally across the head and a comb-marked bun on her neck. Her old body has the narrow waist of a lady. The hands are semi-spoon shape with the exception of a raised thumb section. The molded heelless black shoes which cover the ankles have yellow soles.

No. 183 A, B Just as chinas have acquired names, so have Parians. "Parthenia" has three molded bands painted the same color as the masses of curls.

No. 184 A, B There is a Parian version of Adelina Patti, which appears to have been made from the same molds as the china examples.

No. 185 A, B, C Glass-eyed Parians are not common and are therefor prized. The decorating here varies from the usual Parian style in that the

No. 180

No. 181

No. 182

No. 183A

No. 183B

No. 184A

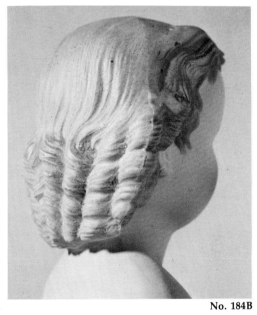

No. 184B

No. 185A

No. 185B

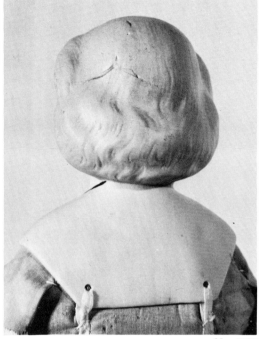

No. 186A

No. 186B

eyebrows are multi-stroke and there are upper and lower eyelashes. The ribbon in her hair is a dark red, which is also unusual. Because intense color must be built of thin painted layers on the unglazed surfaces, each painted layer had to be fired individually; thus dark colors were uncommon. The face is round with full, tinted cheeks. The comb marks in the hair are well defined.

No. 186 A, B Although rare, the glass-eyed Parians are found in several styles. This example has molded earrings, cross necklace, and a blue band.

No. 187 A, B, C Not only does this doll have glass eyes and an elaborate braided hair style, she has a swivel neck which adds to her rare qualities.

No. 188 A, B Another beauty with glass eyes

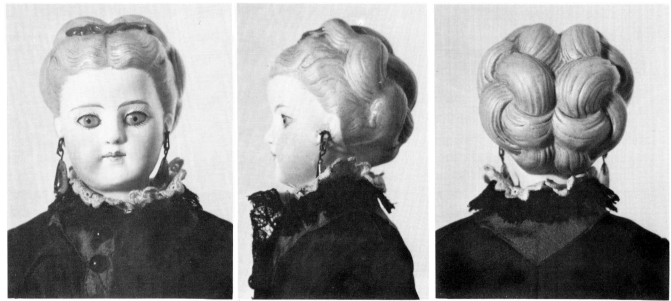

No. 187A

No. 187B

No. 187C

No. 188A

No. 188B

No. 189

has a thinner face and neck. Her hair style consists of a combination of waves, curls, and a braid accented with a bow.

No. 189 The decorating of this Parian is typical except for the color of the hair. Unlike chinas, black-haired Parians are less common than blondes or brunettes. There are red orange lines above the molded upper lid of the eyes, and red dots at the corners of the eyes. The black pupil is painted at the top of the royal blue iris, a style often overlooked by re-producers. There is a white highlight next to the pupils. The molded hair is piled up on top of the head, with puffs of curls on the sides. The back of the hair has eight curls which run horizontally across the head. The brush strokes at the temples are very fine, as if done with a brush that was almost dry. A blue luster band, trimmed with gold, softens the contrast between the black hair and pale complexion.

No. 190 A, B Most Parians seem to be sophisticated ladies. A "Eugenia" with black hair appears rather prim. Her only decorations are a high necked collar and a snood, the same color as her hair. Understated or not, she is truly rare.

No. 191 A, B A similar doll has the more common blond hair. However, the applied ruffle

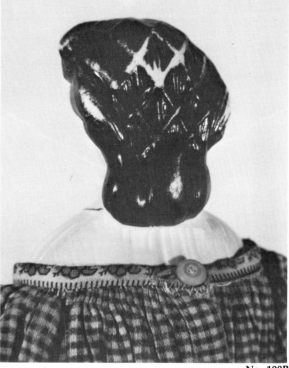

No. 190A

No. 190B

and painted snood would probably attract a novice quicker than the plainer example.

No. 192 A, B Many Parians have a family

resemblance due to the expression on the faces. The decorations create a difference in appearance. This lady has a combination of molded and

No. 191A

No. 191B

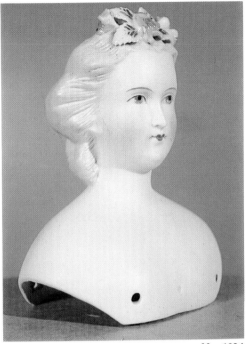

No. 192A

No. 192B

applied decorations. The china glazed ribbon is molded, but the pink rose and white leaves tinted with gold are applied.

No. 193 A, B Three applied pink and yellow

roses nestled in green leaves adorn the curly hair of a Parian with a slender neck.

No. 194 A, B The decorations of this doll include pink flowers and a green molded bow

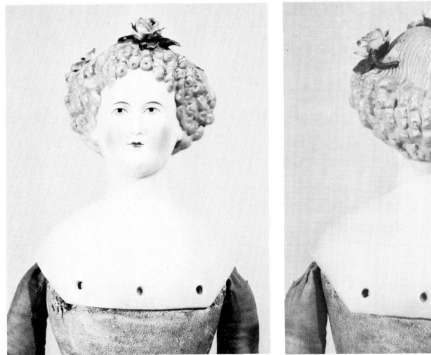

No. 193A

No. 193B

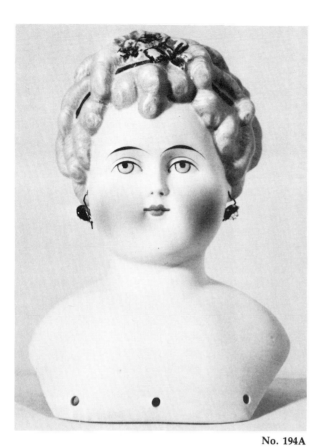

No. 194A   No. 194B

No. 195A   No. 195B

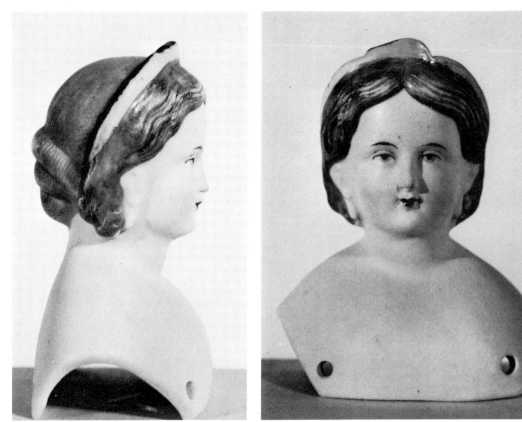

No. 196A   No. 196B

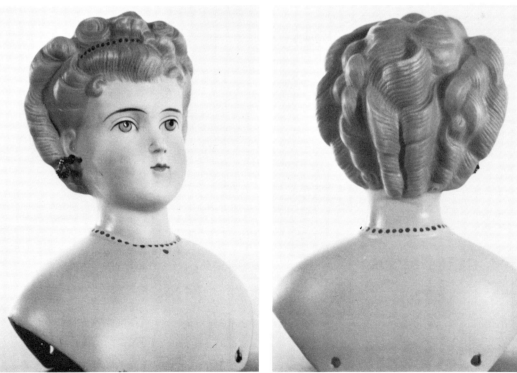

No. 197A   No. 197B

and band. The band disappears in back but the irregular curls are a nice touch.

No. 195 A, B Parians with brown hair are less common than blondes but not as unusual as those with black hair. The rose ribbons, although not applied, compliment the elaborate hair with excellent comb marks.

No. 196 A, B Another brown-haired lass wears an unusual decoration of china trim across her center parted hair. The ornament is glazed

white with black trim. She also has untinted earrings and thick curls gathered at the back.

No. 197 A, B This Parian wears a molded band in her hair and around her neck. Both bands are cleverly painted to appear as individual beads.

No. 198 Parian men are unusual because they seem plain and are not suitable for the fancy ruffles and flowers that are so often used for the sophisticated Parian ladies. The china trim outlined in gold on the collar and tie are the only decoration for this man.

No. 199 A, B The haughty expressions and "too perfect to be real" appearance of many Parians displeases some collectors. This example, has both the elegance of a Parian and the more natural look usually found in the complexion-coated bisque dolls. Details here include lips that are parted in a soft smile, upper and lower eyelashes, ears with realistic molding, and softly curved shoulders. The hair is a soft gray color not usually found in Parian. The only decoration is a narrow green band trimmed with gold luster that goes almost around the head.

Two braids crossed over in back go to a small coronet on the top of the head and three soft waves. She has a straight-legged kid body and lovely complexion coated bisque hands. The doll is named for Pauline, sister of Napoleon.

No. 198

No. 199A

No. 199B

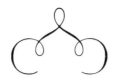

Cloth

Rag or cloth dolls were not regarded as worth collecting until quite recently; collectors preferred bisque which could be washed and easily identified, not some battered old thing with burst seams. Now they are discovering that the scarcity of cloth dolls offers quite a collecting challenge. Part of the scarcity is caused by the apostles of neatness who settle estates, but the most real reason for their limited numbers has been the reluctance of families to part with existing rag dolls for the prices offered. Many rag dolls are fondly remembered by several generations and the sentiment accumulated around these over-loved bundles of cloth and cotton is beyond price. These dolls take no special care, cannot be further damaged, and are just not for sale.

No. 200 The Philadelphia Baby or Sheppard Baby is generally believed to have been made about 1900 for the J. B. Sheppard Company, a Philadelphia department store. This doll is 18 inches tall, smaller than the more common 22-inch size. Because the Sheppard seems never to have any printed trademark or evidence of a pasted label, it apparently sold either without marking or with a string-held tag that was removed.

The Sheppard is made of a fairly coarse grade of off-white knitted underwear material with vertical ribs like purled knitting. At the base of the funnel-like neck, the heavy painted muslin of the head is overcast to the body, apparently by hand. The illustration also shows clearly the arm formation—the doll has no elbow hinge because the shoulder stockinet is sewed to the painted forearm and sheathes the upper arm construction. The doll looks like a boy because of its rugged features. The cheeks are prominent, and the ears are sometimes referred to as "bubble gum." Clearly visible are the common stained feet of the Sheppard. Many of these dolls are found this way in what must have been their original buttoned boots, where the dyes used on the leather boots have bled through to the painted feet. Boots from one Sheppard will exactly match the stains on a barefoot specimen. For comparison a Chase doll is seated by the Sheppard doll.

No. 201 A, B, C The Mothers' Congress Doll, infinitely poorer in material and construction, is not so shy about it origin. Even the patent date,

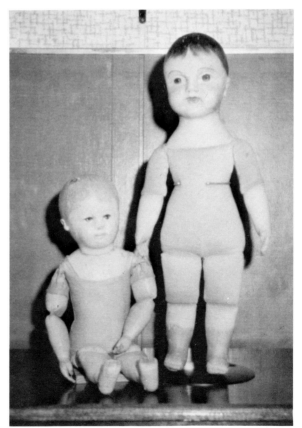

No. 200

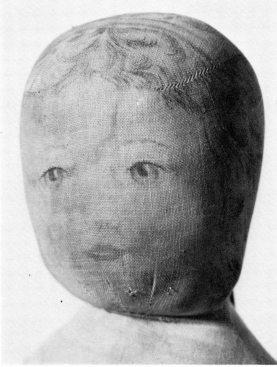

No. 201A

November 6, 1900, is clearly visible in the center panel of the body. Instead of being hand-painted over cloth, the head, shoulders, arms, and legs of this doll are printed on a thin but sturdy grade of muslin. The shoulders, arms, and legs are stippled with red to give the flesh tone. The close-up picture shows part of the seam which almost encircles the head so that it could be flattened like the Sheppard, the Chase, and others. There is also a back seam through the painted hair which leaves the face unmarred except for three darts below the mouth; these give some illusion of a chin—the only concession of any kind to sculptured features.

Although the doll is crude compared to many of the well-known rag dolls, it is nevertheless factory-made. There is hand-stitching where the arms attach to the shoulder stumps and bastings show at the leg attachment; all the rest of the

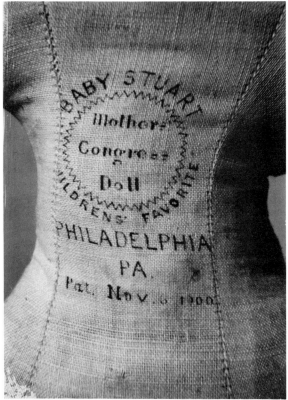

No. 201B

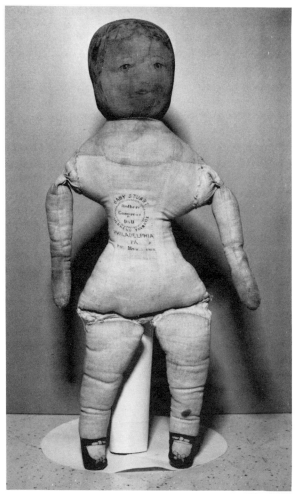

No. 201C

sewing is machine-done with a surprisingly small stitch.

No attempt was made to indicate fingers except for printed red lines; thumbs were ignored. The tiny, printed Mary Jane slippers are black with white bows.

No. 202 One of the early advertising and comic character dolls was designed by Grace Drayton who also illustrated the comic strip. The *Sunday North American,* a Philadelphia newspaper used the rag doll manufactured by the Dolly Company of Philadelphia for promotion of the paper in 1909. The painted face with the round eyes and watermelon mouth resembles the better known Dolly Dingle paper dolls, also created by Grace Drayton. Kaptin Kiddo has a straw hat, orange red mohair wig, blue and white checked cotton costume, and a red belt on which the words, **I'm Kaptin Kiddo** are printed. The original cardboard box has an illustration of the doll. Above the drawing are the words "Kaptin Kiddo, the Hero Doll," below it, the words:

What-Che-Know-Bout-That?
Made for
The Little Friends He Makes
in the
Sunday North American By
The Dolly Company
N.W. Cor 11th and Nine Street
Philadelphia

Copyright
1909 by   Trade Mark
The North American   Registered

Lenci (pronounced "Len-che") of Italy was one of the few commercial firms which recognized that dolls were bought by adult collectors. As early as 1929, ads were directed toward the adult consumer in the United States. The felt Lenci dolls are the ones best remembered. After World War II, the Lenci dolls were made of celluloid, but these never had the appeal of the felt and cloth. However recently felt Lenci dolls were again available in Italy. In 1977 an 18" girl was purchased accompanied by a numbered Certificate.

No. 203 This 9-inch Lenci doll with molded felt face is from the Foreign Country Series. The strip of orange red mohair bangs is sewed to the head and ears by three machine-stitched seams. The rest of the head, covered by the multicolored print scarf, is bald. The gray eyes, which

No. 202

look to the side, are raised; the brown eyelashes are painted with delicate strokes; the sharply raised eyebrows are molded; and the mouth is open as if in surprise.

On the orange felt dress are red dots, sewed

No. 203

with diagonal machine stitching, and a magenta patch sewed by hand. The dress which is attached to the body has not been removed, but the arms and head do not appear jointed as in the case of the larger dolls. The legs are jointed with a hidden attachment. The drawstring pantalets, which are separate, also have a trim of pinked felt. The platform shoes are wooden with felt laces to match the dress. Under her arm the doll carries a wooden pig which is painted pink with blue dots and gray feet; the curled tail is made of felt. The identification includes a silver paper label printed with the words **Lenci Torino, Made in Italy,** and a white and black cloth label which says **Lenci—Made in Italy.**

If a doll has Lenci-type features and a tag saying only ''Made in Italy,'' there is no guarantee that it was made by Lenci. Because many of the close imitators were Italian firms, it is best to consider unidentified Italian cloth dolls as simply an Italian doll of unproved origin.

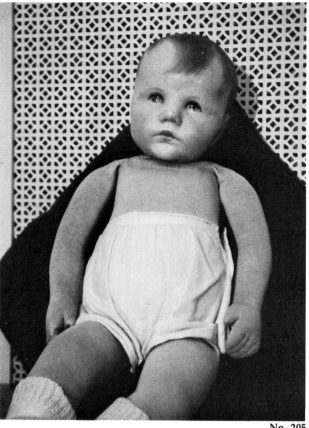

No. 205

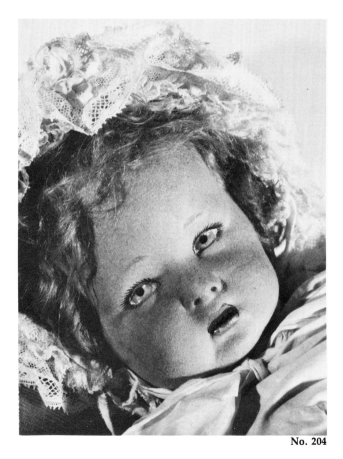

No. 204

No. 204 The Lenci baby has a sweeter expression and more realistic detailed body, the cheeks and chin are softly rounded; multi-stroke eyebrows are in more natural position; and the eyes look straight ahead instead of to the side. The plump face is framed with gently curled mohair; the separate felt fingers and the chunky legs are permanently molded in a life-like position natural to infants. Other Lenci infants were made with less attention to details.

No. 205 This Kathe Kruse infant has a wide-awake look. In the sweet faces of the old dolls such as this one, the eyes were actually portrait-painted. Frau Kruse constantly sketched children at play out in the parks or right in her own studio where they came as visitors. Those sketches were reproduced as dolls, and it is difficult now to find two alike. As with all the older Kruse dolls, this baby has a shy, gentle look. Because of this, Hitler stopped production and ordered many dolls destroyed; he insisted on fearless children with erect postures.

No. 206 Although most of the cloth dolls

No. 206

made by the German artist Kathe Kruse were well received, her experiment with babies proved unsuccessful. This sleeping-eye baby weighed 5-½ pounds! Most of the weight seems to come from sand in his body cavity. While it makes him wonderfully life-like and some pediatricians did buy babies to show young mothers how to handle infants, it also made him too heavy to ship profitably.

The infant heads are made from three pieces of firm, durable cotton cloth. There is a shaping tuck in the face piece where it crosses the crown of the head, and the two back pieces are fitted into it.

The one-piece stockinet baby bodies have leg and arm seams and a hand-stitched seam straight up the back. The arms are shaped and are sewn on at the shoulder, providing for full movement as in the child dolls. There is a life-like sprawl to the infants, accomplished mostly by the fact that the legs are not alike. One leg is fairly straight, but the other knee is turned out and the foot rests on its outer edge. The left foot is numbered: **0713**. This is a European seven with a cross bar like our ''F''.

No. 207 Dolls commemorating special anniversaries or events are always interesting. ''Liberty Belle'' was designed to celebrate the sesquicentennial of our country. A stuffed doll with printed features, the doll is a representation of the Liberty Bell complete with crack. Across the bell dress are printed the words: **150 Years**

of/**American Independence/1776-1926.** Her hat is decorated with her name, stars, and stripes. Annin & Co., New York, N.Y. received a patent on March 23, 1926. A bicentennial edition was produced with 1776-1976 as the date on the skirt.

No. 208 Liberty of London made cloth dolls of historical characters from druids to archbishops. In 1920, when the company registered its trademark, it claimed that the trademark had been used since 1906. During the year of a coronation the principal participants were made. These cloth dolls, made in 1936, represent King George VI and his Queen. It appears that his daughter, Queen Elizabeth II, may be the last royal figure so honored. The dolls have been discontinued for years.

No. 207

No. 208

No. 209

No. 209 Cloth Kewpies were introduced in the 1930s and were highly advertised for several years. The color of this Kewpie is red, but several shades were available. The body has a contour similar to the bisque dolls, with a rounded stomach, chunky legs, and short arms. The hands are shaped like mittens. The projections on the shoulder are the same shade as the rest of the body, but resemble horns instead of wings. The black eyes look to the side and have a white highlight with tiny eyelashes on the top lid. The nose is one round black dot; the mouth has a watermelon shape; and the cheeks are orange red. The top of the cloth head meets at a point, possibly to create the topknot effect.

There are seams in the middle of the front and back of the doll. The cloth tag says:

"Kewpie
Trade Mark Reg. U.S. Pat Office
Pat 1,785,800
Richard G. Krueger, Inc.
New York
Sole Mfg. & Distributors."

Copyright
Rose O'Neill

No. 210 A, B The Alabama Indestructible Baby has a reputation for being a rare doll, yet thousands were produced at the small factory in Roanoke, Alabama. In one year more than 8,000 dolls were produced. Ella Smith, who had come from Georgia, was the originator of the doll. According to sources in Roanoke and old adver-

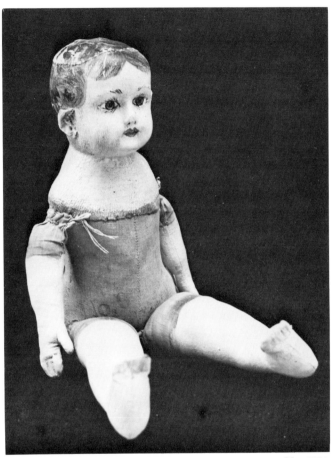

No. 210A

No. 210B

tisements, the doll was first made in 1899. This is several years earlier than collectors have hitherto thought. Mrs. Smith continued to make dolls until her death in 1932.

An act of kindness started her career as a dollmaker. When a neighbor child's beautiful bisque doll was broken, Mrs. Smith offered to repair it. As she worked on the doll she realized the need for a doll that could survive the child's playing. In advertisements the indestructibility of her doll was always emphasized. Many stories have circulated about these dolls. One factory worker claimed that the truck ran over one of them, but didn't even crack the paint, and it was put back into the shipment.

Once when speaking before a group, a frail lady came up after the program and said she

had fond memories of the Ella Smith dolls. When she had to travel to New York alone, she took along an Alabama Baby as a weapon to hit any molester over the head.

The former doll factory was years ago converted into an apartment building. But in February 1975 an historical marker was finally placed at the site. No.210A is unusual for instead of blue or brown painted shoes (as seen in No.210B) it was designed to have separate shoes. Stamped on back is the mark Mrs. S S Smith Manufacturer Roanoke Alabama.

No. 211 The close-up demonstrates the typical decorating style of the Alabama Indestructible Baby, because every doll was painted by hand, there is always a slight variation. In the early examples the ears were sewn to the head. Later, staples were used.

No. 212 More modern dolls also have enthusiastic admirers. "Eloise" more closely resembles the little girl Eloise in the book than many dolls designed to represent book characters. The doll was made in the late 1950s by the Hollie Toy Co.

No. 213 Cloth advertising dolls make interesting additions to collections. Not only do they reflect trends in our culture but the initial investment is minimal. When an edition is discontinued, most of them rise in value. One of the problems with collecting such dolls is distinguishing between an original and a reissue. Often the same design is used.

The Eskimo Pie Dolls do have a different design, although the mailing bags have the same Post Office Box number and identical printing.

Here's another kind of
ESKIMO Pleasure-Pak

containing your . . .ESKIMO
Brand
R A G   D O L L

For Best Results:

Open and protect it immediately in the warm arms of a loving child.

The original doll, first issued in 1962 (on the left), has black eyes and hair, brown top, and black pants. The newer issue, available in 1975, has brown hair, blue eyes, red top, and brown pants; **eskimo pie** printed across the front.

No. 211

No. 212

No. 213

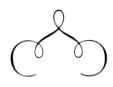

American Composition

There are almost as many definitions for composition as there are collectors. The dictionary definition of composition is too vague for practical use. The idea that papier mâché and composition differ by the proportion of ingredients used is also confusing. Perhaps the most simple and direct description of composition is "papier mâché with a varnished finish." In 1908, these sometimes called stepchildren of the doll world were once heralded as the "dolls of the future." The main selling point seems to have been that many were American-made and unbreakable. Butler Brothers claimed: "You can pound one against the counter, drop on the floor or throw across the room without breaking it." Not only was this statement an exaggeration, but time has given many compositions an imperfect finish. Age has proved an even harsher enemy to these dolls than eager children.

Many collectors are surprised to learn that composition was sometimes more expensive than the now preferred bisque. In the 1921 Butler Brothers catalog, 9-inch bisque Kewpies sold for 20 cents a dozen less than the same size in composition.

In the early 20th century, American dolls were an unimportant part of the market. The "Can't Break Dolls"—a trade name for a type of composition—had been made as early as 1900, but were not successful. American dolls seemed destined for obscurity until Florence Pretez, in 1908, copyrighted a whimsical creature called Billiken, which gave the American doll business its first big break. These sold well and in 1909, the Horsman Company combined the Billiken fad with the Teddy Bear craze by putting the head of the statute on a soft, Teddy Bear-type body. In

six months, 200,000 had been sold, establishing Billiken as one of the best selling dolls. The Billiken's claim that it brought good luck was at least true for the domestic manufacturers. American companies were quick to detect a trend and produced numerous characters, including dolls inspired by the comic strips. The boycott of German products during World War I gave American dolls an extra boost.

By 1916, the compositions did indeed appear to be the dolls of the future, as claimed eight years earlier. Butler Brothers even featured a color page of American-made unbreakable dolls. The dolls were dressed as cowboys, Indians, soldiers, Santa Claus, and babies complete with celluloid rattles. The characters included Baby Grumpy, Gene Carr Kids, and Dutch Campbell boys.

After the war German bisques were again available in the United States but the doll market had changed. There was now a strong anti-German sentiment. For a time Butler Brothers and *Playthings*, a trade publication for dolls and toys, refused to carry advertisements of German goods.

The American companies put up $65,000 for a mass advertising campaign to educate the public to the superiority of the American dolls. One of the main themes was "Avoid a childhood tragedy—the broken doll" in which little girls were pictured crying, holding broken bisque dolls. Another emphasized that American dolls were "made by" Americans who helped free the world.

Composition continued to be the most popular material for American manufacturers until 1939 when Ideal introduced with much fanfare

No. 214

No. 215

an all-plastic doll. (The *New York Times* wrote an article as a news event.) The commercial appeal of composition steadily dropped from that time.

No other material, though, had reflected the trends in American society as thoroughly as did composition. Popular styles and personalities were quickly imitated in the doll world.

No. 214 Charlie Chaplin was one of the earliest of the movie stars to be represented by a composition doll. The likeness is excellent and superior to the celebrity dolls that were produced in the 1930s. This 14-inch doll has dark molded hair, one stroke eyebrows, intaglio eyes which look to the side, straight thin nose, black moustache, and a mouth with a serious expression. His original clothing includes brown plaid pants, white shirt, black tie and coat. The cloth body and the black cloth feet are stuffed with straw. Still sewn on some of the coats are the words

CHARLIE CHAPLIN DOLL
WORLD'S GREATEST COMEDIAN
Made Exclusively By Louis Amberg & Son N.Y.
By Special Arrangement with Essany Film Co.

Another doll almost identical is marked on the back of the neck **A.D. Co.** Not all Charlie Chaplins were advertised by name. In 1916, a doll with a moustache and resembling Charlie Chaplin was called "Funny Boy." Its wholesale price was $1.55.

No. 215 This doughboy soldier, called the "Liberty Boy," reflects the strong national pride of the World War I era. The molded uniform is quite authentic in its detail, including sergeant's stripes on the sleeve and wrapped woolen leggings. The color of the uniform is army brown with black tie and buttons. The doll has blue eyes and molded hair, painted a sandy color. On the back a little above the waist the doll is marked with the word **Ideal** in a diamond shape. The height of the doll is 12 inches.

No. 216 Although unmarked, this doll is regarded as American because the clothes represent that of an American soldier of World War I. The cloth uniform is authentic brown with a black tie. Unlike the Ideal doll, this one has more childlike look, with a rounder face, pug nose, rosebud mouth, and curly molded hair. The shoes are also molded. The height is 12 inches.

No. 216

No. 217 A, B In 1921, Butler Brothers described the Kewpies as "the biggest selling dolls on the market." Kewpies were created from the drawings of the American artist and poet, Rose O'Neill, who said the original Kewpie figures were inspired by a dream. Composition Kewpies were first made in 1913; bisque ones had been made in 1912. An early example of composition, this 12-inch doll has the one-piece torso jointed only at the shoulders. As in the drawings, the doll has hands with a starfish shape and tiny blue wings on its shoulders. Many of the compositions were dressed in various outfits, including sweaters, ribbon skirts, and fancy dresses. The 12-inch size bride sold for $16.50 per dozen as compared to $7.50 a dozen for the undressed Kewpie.

According to Rowena Ruggles, author of *The One Rose*, Cameo Doll Company in 1933, started producing a swivel-neck composition Kewpie without wings although the face, topknot and starfish-shaped hands remained the same.

No. 218 A "Scootles," copyrighted in 1930, is another creation by Rose O'Neill. The doll is based on the "Baby Tourist" which appears in the Kewpieville series. Although the Negro Scoo-

No. 218A

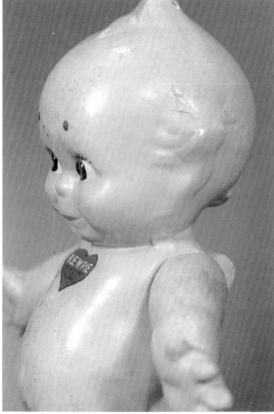

No. 217A

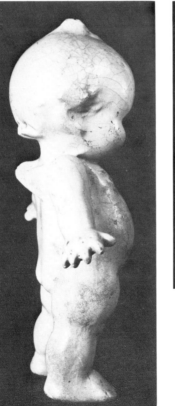

No. 217B

No. 218B

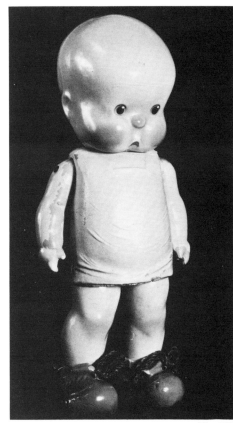

No. 219

tles is not as common as the white, it is not considered rare because thousands were produced. The price range of Scootles was from 79 cents to $12.

No. 218 B Joseph Kallas, owner of Cameo Co., much associated with the production of Rose O'Neill creations, made other interesting dolls. **Margie,** copyrighted by Joseph Kallas in 1929, has an unusual face. Her head is composition. The body with joints at elbows, knees and ankles, is made of wood.

No. 219 The "HeBee-SheBee" dolls, copyrighted by Horsman in 1925, have a unique design. The bald head with a swivel neck has blue intaglio eyes, turned down mouth, a button nose, and round cheeks painted bright orange with white highlight. The only clothing on this 10-½-inch HeBee is a white molded chemise full of wrinkles, and blue booties; the SheBee has pink booties. The arms and legs are jointed

though movement of the legs is restricted by the chemise. The paint on HeBee-SheBee was not durable, so peeling on the arms is not unexpected. The doll is based on a creation by Charles Twelvetrees.

No. 220 In 1926, the Patsy doll by the Effanbee Company became a trend setter and another American success story. Patsy was advertised as "The Personality Doll, The Miss of a Million Moods, Every Pose a Picture." For the first time separate wardrobes were available and strongly promoted, and this new concept helped stabilize the American doll industry by encouraging sales of doll dresses throughout the year instead of purchases just at Christmastime. The Effanbee Company also organized a Patsy fan club in which members received newsletters four times a year describing many Effanbee dolls. The idea is still popular and is used by Mattel. The 14-inch doll here is marked **Patsy** on the head and **Patricia** and **Effanbee** on the body. Patsy has a small closed mouth which collectors describe as

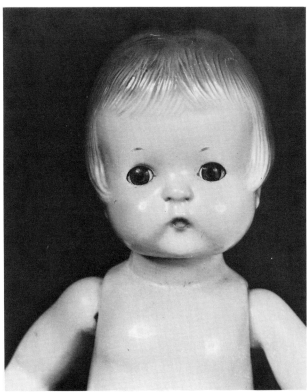

No. 220

rosebud, short molded hair, sleeping eyes of brown, and synthetic eyelashes. In 1938, Effanbee was still advertising Patsys.

No. 221 Appropriately marked **Wee Patsy** this doll, also by Effanbee, is 5½ inches tall. She has the typical Patsy look, bobbed hair with bangs, painted blue eyes, and a rosebud mouth. Her hair has good comb marks and a molded band painted the same reddish brown color as her hair. Unlike the larger doll, she has no eyebrows or eyelashes. The torso of the body is well shaped, but lacks detail molding of the buttocks, a characteristic of many Patsys. She has molded socks and black painted shoes, a feature the 14-inch Patsy does not have. The composition appears to be a better grade because the finish is still in excellent condition. The French copied Patsy in celluloid and the Germans copied her in bisque, good evidence that the Patsy line made an impact on the world doll market.

No. 222 "Lamkin" is not as realistically

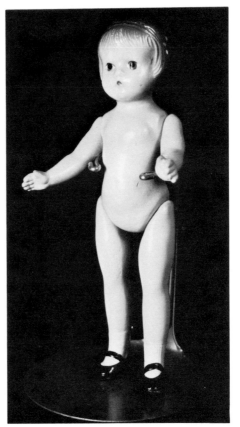

No. 221

made as the Bye-Lo, but its character look is more suitable to composition. The stuffed flesh color body simulates the feel of a cuddly baby and makes holding the doll almost irresistable. The eyes are green with red dots at the corner. The decoration includes upper and lower eyelashes but lacks eyebrows. The hair is muted sandy color. Inside the red orange mouth is a felt tongue. The arms and legs have rolls of fat and dimples; on a finger of the left hand is a molded and painted gold baby ring. Effanbee advertised Lamkin in 1930.

No. 223 A, B Dewees Cochran, an imaginative American artist, decided that children would enjoy having dolls that resembled themselves. She developed several basic face shapes that along with correct color of hair and eyes would create the effect of a portrait doll. Approximately 50,000 of these dolls were sold through the Effanbee Company. In 1939, the dolls were featured as cover story for *Life* magazine. This is a

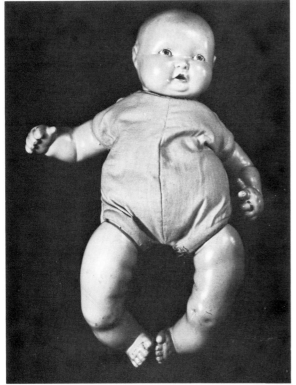

No. 222

No. 223A

No. 223B

good barometer of the impact that the dolls made. The dolls were called "America's Children, Look-alike, and Portrait dolls."

No. 224 A, B This is another example of Dewees Cochran "America's Children."

No. 225 A, B Boys were also made by De-

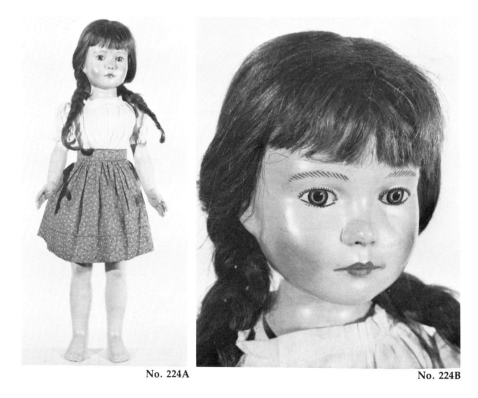

No. 224A

No. 224B

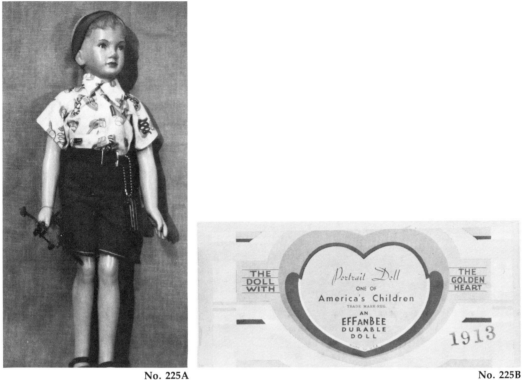

No. 225A   No. 225B

wees Cochran: an Effanbee's label shown, the stamped "1913" is the stock number, not a date.

No. 226 A, B In 1939, Effanbee created three

sets of 30 dolls representing the history of our country. This expensive collection, costing $30,000, toured throughout our nation. The heads used for these dolls were made from the America's Children series designed by Dewees

No. 226A

No. 226B

Cochran. The costumes covered the centuries from the early beginning of our country to 1939. These approximately 20-inch dolls were eventually sold. The mass-produced version of these dolls was available in a smaller size with different face and less elaborate clothes. The example illustrated is one of the three original dolls designed to represent the Virignia Colony of 1608.

No. 227 Although the mass-produced version of the historical dolls originally sold for $5, they are prized collectors items now. This example, dressed in an off-white costume trimmed with lace, represents 1760. Collectors should be thankful that because of the six inches difference in the height between the limited and mass-produced version, the dolls will not be easily confused.

In determining the current value of a composition doll, sentiment or special appeal seems to be more important than a doll's scarcity.

Shirley Temple was the most successful of all compositions and many are available, yet the prices on Shirley seem to be high when compared with other dolls of the same material. A survey conducted by *Toy World* magazine, revealed that this was the doll with the highest volume of sales in June 1935. By 1937, the third

year of production, sales had already reached $3 million. That year it continued to be Ideal Company's best seller. In April 1939, the manufacturer was still advertising Shirley Temple as the "Number 1 box office today." However, in the later 1939 ads, Ideal made no mention of the Shirley Temple dolls.

No. 228 In 1934, Ideal introduced a doll to represent the popular child star, Shirley Temple. Marked on the head and body **Shirley Temple, Ideal,** the doll also has her original box with a facsimile of her hand-printed name on the label. The tin eyes move from side to side, or flirt, a process which required 84 manufacturing steps. Shirley's wardrobe, which was even more extensive than Patsy's many designs, was based on the roles she had played in the movies. The later dolls came with curlers and were advertised with the slogan "Keep Shirley Curly." To promote the doll, Shirley Temple Resemblance Contests were held, and some department stores even gave big prizes such as ponies and trips to Hollywood. Stores often made Shirley Temple's birthday a special event with entertainment and refreshments. Another scheme was to give a free gift to

No. 227

No. 228

every girl who brought a Shirley Temple doll to the store.

Retail prices for the Shirley Temple doll ranged from $2.49 for the 11-inch size to about $12 for the 27-inch doll. Separate dresses sold for 94 cents to $2.49.

Aside from her wig, the doll has little resemblance to the child star who delighted so many millions. On a television talk show in May 1972, Shirley Temple commented that the color of the doll's eyes was wrong, because her own eyes are brown.

Unfortunately, there is a tendency for the doll's composition to crack and craze. The tin eyes often develop a starburst effect similar in appearance to a blind eye. However, an occasional drop of sewing machine oil returns such eyes to their original condition.

No. 229 The 18-inch Baby Shirley Temple was introduced in 1935, a year after the first Shirley. The doll is attractive, but was not as heavily promoted and did not sell as well. Because many collectors prefer the baby, its price is usually higher than the typical Shirley Temple. The composition curved arms and bent legs are chunky. The body is cloth with a cry box (it no longer works in this particular doll). Her factory-original bonnet and dress are made of pink organdy, trimmed with white lace.

No. 230 A, B Not all compositions are made to represent children. When looking at fortune telling ''Sibyl'' a Hallowe'en witch naturally comes to mind. Sibyl's face is withered, her hands are gnarled, her back is hunched. On her black blouse are the traditional designs associated with sorcery: cats, witches, stars, hearts, clovers, and diamonds. The signs of the Zodiac are printed on her cardboard base, and the paper skirt of multi-colored fortunes is intact.

The method for revealing the fortune is unusual and complicated. Instead of merely plucking a fortune out of the skirt, one must select a question from the eight-page instruction booklet. Remembering the color of the page, one then whirls the doll while the base remains stable. A fortune the same color as the question page is chosen among those which stop on the proper Zodiac sign. These novel directions are printed on the booklet which accompanies Sibyl:

If the truth you wish to hear,
Give my base a quarter turn,

No. 229

No. 230A

No. 230B

No. 231

Find your question in this book
On its *number* closely look
The color too just keep in mind
When on the base your birthmonth find
On nearest fold of sefsame [sic] hue
Find your answer clear and true!

On her cylinder box are printed the words **Sibyl Fortune Teller Patents applied for. Sibyl Fortune Teller Co., Los Angeles.** The instruction book includes a street address and a telephone number with only five digits; however there is no record of a patent having been received.

No. 231 Jointed only at the shoulders, this doll has a black mohair wig and painted features

which are described as roughish; her large eyes look to the side, and the red mouth is small. All composition, she has molded white socks and black shoes. Although unmarked, she matches the type of doll described as "The Flirt" advertised in the 1932 issue of Butler Brothers catalog. The only apparent variation is in height; this doll is 12 inches; the one advertised is about half that size. The price of the doll in the catalog is 85 cents a dozen, the lowest price for composition listed that year by Butler Brothers. According to the ad, the doll "sold in large quantities in variety stores throughout the country."

No. 232 In all-original condition, this plump

No. 232

No. 233

18-inch doll is a perfect stereotype of an old time Negro Mammy. The brown face has many African features, including the broad flattened nose, prominent cheeks, and full, smiling lips which reveal large white teeth. Unfortunately, the composition of her face is deteriorating. Hoop earrings are attached to the black mohair wig, which is covered by a red and white bandana. The head is tilted back as if she is enjoying a hearty joke. The factory-made dress of red and white cotton print has ruffles at the neck and sleeves. The fat curved arms seem out of proportion as do the legs with the molded shoes with laces. The bottom of each shoe is hollow, indicating that at one time the doll may have had a special stand. The brown cloth body is firm, and the shape is similar to that of a French Fashion. It has a "V" shaped waist and a bottom that is sewn with three seams. Printed on a gold tag are the words **Tony Sarg's Mammy Doll, sole distributor, Geo.**

Borgfeldt Corp., N.Y., N.Y. There are no marks on the doll. Tony Sarg was a famous puppeteer and an author of a number of children's books. He also designed marionettes for the Alexander Doll Company and Walt Disney.

No. 233 Of all the commercially manufactured Indian dolls, most collectors feel that "Skookum" dolls portrayed the American Indian with the most dignity. The first commercial Skookum doll heads were made in 1913 of dried apples. This group of Indians is representative of the composition dolls designed by Mary McAvoy. According to Kimport, the Skookums were made until the 1960s. The later dolls have feet made of plastic instead of composition, cloth, or wood.

No. 234 This doll, called **Jo Jo,** is marked with his name and **(C) 1937 Horsman.** The baby has green sleeping eyes of metal, synthetic upper lashes, lower painted lashes, one-stroke eyebrows, and a bright orange mouth. The composition torso has a molded navel; the legs are slightly bent, and the kneecaps are blushed with orange. The 12-inch doll does not actually resemble a baby, which is typical of this period.

No. 234

No. 235

According to a 1936 article in *Fortune Magazine,* American manufacturers during the 1930s held the opinion that no doll should look like a real child.

No. 235 Even the trends in music were reflected in the doll world, as illustrated by these Bobbie-Mae dolls which were designed to "swing and sway with Sammy Kaye." Although both of these examples are dressed in blue, the molded dress came in a variety of colors. The collar, buttonns, and sashes are painted white. The shoes, with a molded strap, are solid white, as are the socks. The doll with the coffee brown complexion has black hair decorated with reddish brown bows; the other has carrot red hair and white bows. Both have painted eyes which look to the side, long eyelashes, and smiling lips. The swaying motion is created by wooden beams to which metal rods are attached.

Inside each doll's body is a stationary wooden beam through which a pivotal metal rod is attached to the skirt. In the head there is a mobile beam through which a swinging rod is attached. The separate beams and rods allow the head and body to sway in opposite directions.

No. 236 The Campbell's Kid Dolls were

No. 236

No. 237A

No. 237B

based on the drawings by Grace Drayton, although Joseph Campbell held the copyright. Many companies have made Campbell's Kids, but the first were made by Horsman. Over a period of years, Horsman produced several models. This doll resembles one sketched in a pamphlet published by Horsman. The boy of the 1940s wears a chef's hat, a one-piece blue jumper, and an apron. The girl in the series had a white dress and in her hair was glued a red bow.

The painted eyes which look to the side have heart-shaped pupils. Other interesting features included molded eyebrows, pug nose, and watermelon smile. Printed on the label attached to the jumper are the words:

Campbell's Kid,
A Horsman Doll,
Permission of Campbell Soup Company

The tomato soup can on the label is made of felt.

No. 237 A, B These Dionne Quintuplets are distinguished from each other only by gold plated pins bearing their individual names. They have black human hair wigs, round faces, and dark sleeping eyes and are dressed in pastel colors of yellow, green, pink, and blue. The 12-inch toddler size which represents the Dionne sisters at the age of two, is unusual and harder to obtain than the smaller dolls. The Dionne dolls were

No. 239

No. 238

first introduced in 1935, though the copyright for the Quintuplets was not obtained until 1936. By 1937 more than a million dolls had been sold. The Alexander Company's ads called the Dionne girls "Nature's finest example of healthy happy childhood." The nurse of the real life Quints, Yvonne Lerous, made public appearances for the Alexander Company to increase sales. The firm, borrowing an idea from Ideal, recommended that stores use the Quints' birthday for profitable promotion. The live Quints were so publicized by the news media that the dolls sold well in such foreign countries as South Africa.

No. 238 Designed to represent Scarlett O'Hara, this doll, by Madame Alexander, is 17 inches tall. She has a black human hair wig, green eyes, dark red lips, and a pointed chin. Her antebellum print dress with green trim has a hoop skirt which accents her waist. The green shoes without high heels are another authentic style of the pre-Civil War period. Pinned on the dress in the shape of a book is a gold locket, with the words **Gone With The Wind.** The doll originally sold from $2.95 to $6.95. Many department stores, such as Rich's of Atlanta, promoted the doll with special advertising and displays.

No. 239 Dolls dressed as nuns were popular subjects during the 1930s. The doll's habit, underclothes, and shoes are black. The painted blue eyes and small mouth give the face a doll-like appearance. The religious accoutrements include a rosary and a crucifix with the word **France** impressed on the back. This 13-inch doll is unmarked and difficult to identify. A company called "Mme. Louise of Syracuse" made religious dolls designed by Marguerite Davis. This company claimed to have pioneered the idea of religious dolls. However, there were several other manufacturers which made nun dolls, including

Schranz & Bieber, which advertised that it imported the rosaries from France.

No. 240 The Geo. Borgfeldt Corporation reissued the Bye-Lo in an unbreakage composition and sleeping eyes. The doll designed by Grace Storey Putnam was originally made in wax and bisque to represent a three-day old baby. The company hoped the Bye-Lo would still have the same phenomenal appeal that it had possessed in the 1920s, but little girls of the 1940s seemed to prefer the drinking and wetting baby dolls.

Collectors have assumed from a statement of Mrs. Putnam's which appeared in *The Fascinating Story of Dolls* that the composition Bye-Lo was first sold in 1934 for she wrote:

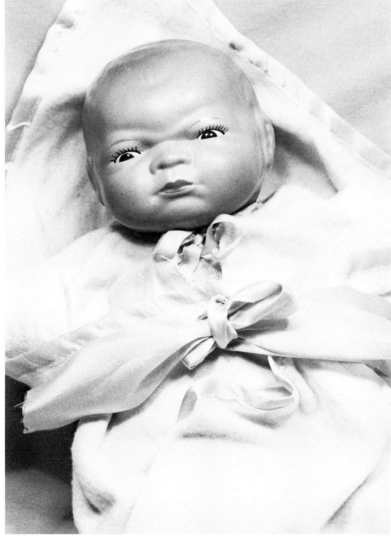

No. 240

"In 1934 . . . Borgfeldt decided to bring back the Bye-Lo baby in composition . . . . But just as the doll was ready to reappear the Shirley Temple doll came on the market and took the country by storm."

However, an article in the August 1938 issue of *Playthings* discusses the composition Bye-Lo as a new product. Mrs. Putnam must have meant that plans in 1934 were discontinued.

The price range of the Bye-Lo was 97 cents to $1.95, which made it relatively inexpensive when compared to many of the personality dolls. The current interest in dolls designed by outstanding artists seems to have increased the price of the composition Bye-Lo over other originally more expensive dolls.

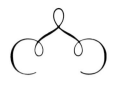

Schoenhut

Though Schoenhut dolls are not yet considered antique since they were made in the 20th century, they are considered collectible. The durable nature is perhaps one reason Schoenhut dolls are fairly easy to locate today. As with all wooden dolls, they are not easily destroyed, though on many the enamel paint has deteriorated.

With this in mind, a collector when buying, should always check to see whether the paint has been retouched. In some instances all the old paint has been scraped off and the head is entirely repainted. Newer paint generally has a fresher cleaner look, while the original paint has signs of aging, such as discoloration or crazing. Schoenhut dolls do not require any special care, but they should *never* be stored under fluorescent lights, or the paint will bubble and crack.

The Schoenhuts with all-wooden heads are, at the moment, preferred to the ones with wigs. The dolls with molded wooden hair were the first made, but both varieties were manufactured into the 1930s.

No. 241 This all-wooden head boy is 15-½ inches tall. He has a laughing open mouth with two upper and two lower teeth. The expression is similar to some of the Gerbruder Heubachs. The black molded hair has good comb marks, indicating naturally curly hair. The blue intaglio eyes are a little small in proportion to the rest of the face. The eyes have black pupils and white highlights. His companion is a large Schoenhut poodle with painted eyes and carved fur; the white paint is in excellent condition. Schoenhut animals often find a place in doll collections. The poodle is 8 inches long; the scale seems large when compared to other Schoenhut animals. The brown eyes have intaglio pupils with white high-

lights. The white tail made of cord has three rows of fringe to indicate fluffy fur.

No. 242 A, B A girl with a brown mohair wig has a less expressive face. The dewigged Schoenhut beside her shows the jointed wooden body. There are Schoenhut markings on both the head and body. The two holes at the bottom of the feet are for the special Schoenhut metal stand. The shoes and stockings have two holes in the soles to match those in the feet and stand. This stand had the advantage of never disturbing the clothes, because it fitted into the feet.

No. 241

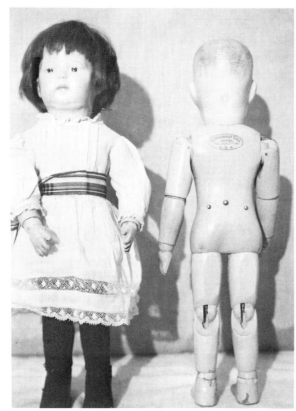

No. 242A

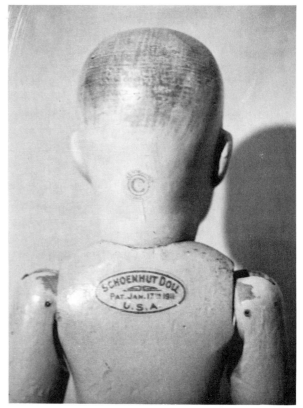

No. 242B

The Schoenhut Humpty Dumpty circus started in 1903 with jointed clowns, named Humpty , Dumpty, and Cracker-Jack, which sold for a dollar. Animals were also available in limited numbers. As the demand for the circus increased, so did the characters and animals. Many brightly colored accessories, including pedestals with pasted decals were added to the line, Among the imaginative accoutrements were a spinning bowl and stick, (balanced by whirling the stick), American flags, balls, whips, hoops, and weights. There was even a collapsible canvas tent with a sawdust ring. The 24-½ by 24-½-inch ring weighed five pounds.

The circus was advertised as having 10,001 outstanding tricks. Certainly the possibility of different combinations added to the pleasure of collecting. In 1931 Butler Brothers was selling a 10-piece circus set for $2.00 and a 12-piece set for $3.00. As with other American-made playthings,

No. 243

the value of the circus figures continues to increase even though they were mass-produced for years.

No. 243 The clowns come in two sizes, dressed in one-piece cotton and silk costumes. The smaller size was recommended for younger children. Although the clown was one of the original items, there was no important change in its design during the years. Evidently the company prided itself on tradition, and in the 1920s the idea was stressed that children could play with toys exactly like the ones their parents had possessed as children. Of course, little change meant less expense for the Schoenhut Company. The illustrations in the catalogue showed the clown in various contortionist positions. The clowns had a jointed head, jointed arms and legs, plus joints at the feet to aid in balancing.

Examples shown have their original white cotton costumes with red dots and stripes. The faces are decorated with red and black paint. The

No. 245

wide mouths are smiling with white painted teeth showing. The ears, made of separate pieces of wood, were often victims of rough play. Aside from the paint and ears, the clowns have lived up to the advertising claim that they were remarkably durable.

No. 244 This example suggests that the clowns' heads may sometimes have been made out of bisque. The design appears to be identical to the wooden ones. If not made by Schoenhut, it certainly is a faithful imitation.

No. 245 The brown horse advertised as "educated" has a white blaze on the head and four white-stockinged feet. The ears are made of leather; the mane is simply part of the wooden body painted black. The tail is of brown string. The horses came with leather saddles which are removable. The Negro Dude is the rider.

No. 246 The elephant is well-shaped and painted a realistic gray. The ears are of leather. The legs are jointed at the ankle to give more dexterity; the smaller version of the elephant

No. 244

No. 246

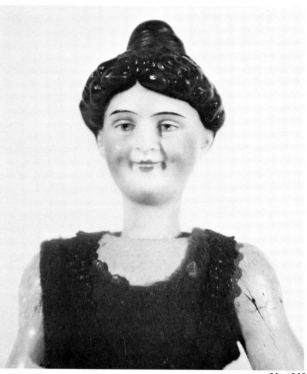

No. 248

No. 247

lacks this feature, indicating that some expensive details were thought unnecessary for younger children.

No. 247 The lion from Schoenhut's "Humpty Dumpty Menagerie of Wild Beasts" has more details than many of the animals. In some animals, such as the mule, the features are exaggerated to give a cartoon effect, but this is not evident in the lion. In his coat there are shadings of color, which is also unusual. The cord tail is plaited.

No. 248 This lady acrobat has the standard Schoenhut body but a bisque head. The bisque head ones are considered prizes. The doll came with both light and dark hair. The smiling mouth is open-closed; the molded hair with a topknot has well shaped curls. She has red lines above the eyes which dispels the myth that this decorating style was not used after 1900.

No. 249

No. 249 The man acrobat has a handlebar mustache and thick curly hair. He also can balance on the tightrope.

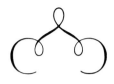

A Variety of Dolls

The dolls discussed so far have been made of the materials in great demand by collectors. Novices often overlook equally interesting dolls available in less popular varieties. If a doller does not feel compelled to follow the crowd, a rare doll can sometimes be obtained for the price of a more common example in a currently preferred material.

Bonnet Dolls

Bonnet dolls were rarely favorites of children because their hair and hats could not be rearranged. Most bonnets are made of a coarser quality bisque than Parian, though like Parian they lack a complexion coat. As with other varieties, "bonnet" was not always the term used in the old mail order catalogs. In 1890, the Butler Brothers wholesale catalog referred to the dolls as "hooded" dolls. In later years they were called "fancy hatted," even "princess" dolls.

Although some bonnet dolls were made in the 1860s and 1870s, the majority were made in the last decade of the 19th century and the early part of the 20th century. The Butler Brothers catalog of 1888 described the china limb doll with a hood as a new doll. The 8-inch example sold for 43 cents a dozen, and the 11-inch specimen was priced at 85 cents a dozen. By 1916, Butler Brothers was no longer advertising hatted dolls, with the exception of small all-bisques.

No. 250 A, B Bonnet dolls did not always reflect the styles in current vogue. The hat was obviously inspired by the Puritan heritage. It is gray with black and gold trim and is tilted slightly over one eye. The hair has a faint suggestion of curls but lacks comb marks. Many

No. 250A

No. 250B

No. 251A

No. 251B

collectors enjoy collecting boy bonnet dolls to escort their ladies.

No. 251 A, B The inspiration for this young girl appears to be a figurine, perhaps popular around the turn of the century. However, there are two sew holes front and back assuring us that the head was intended to be used as a doll. A white space was left between the lips, creating an unusual expression for a bonnet doll.

No. 252 This doll resembles a 15-inch example advertised by Butler Brothers as "Our Quarter 1890 Hooded Doll" at $2.15 a dozen. Butler Brothers describes the hooded dolls as novelties, so apparently they were not a stable part of the doll market. This doll has a molded collar with raised dots painted with gold. The paint is wearing—a common condition. The cap is blue, but this style has been found in other colors.

No. 253 This example has a much detailed stocking cap with the desirable glazed or china trim on the tassel of the stocking cap and the bow tie at the neck. The gold trim on the doll cannot be washed off, indicating that the gold paint was fired. The cap, with two shades of pink instead of one, also indicates extra work. The heavy eyebrows and large eyes give the doll a mas-

No. 252

No. 253

culine look. The round collar, bow tie and shirt lapels further illustrate a style for a boy. On the shoulder is the mark **S.** When his old cotton stuffed body was removed from the head for repair, a yellowed scrap of paper was found with the words **A Seth Doll.** The original owner could give no clue to its meaning. The hair has comb marks that suggest a windblown style. The pink shoes match the color of the cap. The soles of the shoes are painted the same color as the tops, an economy measure that is in contrast to the number of work hours spent on the head.

No. 254 A, B While this doll is attractive, there are indications that it was made for the economy market, even though the decorating of the face was done by a talented artist. The entire back of the head from the top of the billowy bonnet to the bottom of the shoulder plate is left undecorated. The only tinting on her bonnet and below the neck consists of one green and one pink bow. The color of the blond hair is so faint that it almost appears as a watercolor wash.

Nos. 255 A, B, 256 Comparing a reproduction with an original is always interesting. **No. 256** right, is an excellent reproduction marked by the artist **Brouse.** The detail in the reproduction is less distinct and the bisque has a smoother texture than in the original. Both use the colors pink, green, and blond for bonnet and hair. The original also has a gold knot for trim on the bow.

No. 257 Dolls with flowers and insects, such as dragon flies, appeared in 1901. The butterfly

No. 255A

No. 255B

No. 254A

No. 254B

No. 256

doll either had a paper sticker or was not originally imported to this country.

No. 258 A, B Most bonnets are marked but with only a size number or country of origin, making it almost impossible to identify the factory which made them. We believe this unusual mobcap bonnet doll was made by Kestner. The blue threaded glass eyes resemble those that are

seems to be the most easily found. Like other bonnets, it came in several colors. The wings are speckled with two shades of pink, with some areas left untinted. Though this doll was made after the 1890 law requiring that all imported dolls be marked with the country of origin, she bears no mark indicating a country. Perhaps the

No. 258A

No. 257

No. 258B

found in Kestner dolls. The mouth has the square ends which indicate that the painting was done with a stencil as a guide, a practical method used by Kestner to enable anyone, not just an artist, to do the decorating. The incised number, **10545,** on the shoulder is similar to many Kestner serial numbers.

The blue molded bonnet has a double ruffle above the forehead and teal blue ribbons with bows at the brim line. Each ribbon has trailer streamers which reach the tousled blond curls. The cloth hair-stuffed body has leather arms and maroon kid shoes. The shoes have sewed-on heels, a style not popular until the late 1860s. The cloth legs are dark teal.

Papier-Mâché

Papier mâché, literally "chewed paper," has varying ingredients to increase its strength. Technically it could be classified as a composition but the term composition is usually is reserved for dolls with a varnished surface.

Over the years many collectors have come to use Eleanor St. George's term "milliner models" to designate early papier-mâché with elaborate hair style, thin wooden limbs, and the narrow kid bodies of the 1820s to the 1840s. Her choice of the name apparently was due to the belief that the dolls were originally designed to display fashions; the term is misleading because subsequent research has revealed so-called milliner model dolls in very plain original clothing. It is unlikely that any of the recently suggested names such as "coiffeur models" will be widely used. Until the United States government changed its regulation that an article had be be made before 1830 to be classified an antique, a majority of the aristocratic milliner models were among the limited varieties of dolls that qualified for the term.

No. 259 A, B This milliner's model has a stiff kid body with a narrow waist and long thin arms; legs are of wood. The hair is parted in the middle, puffed on the sides with an elaborate braided bun at the neck. The slim neck is appropriate for the deeply molded shoulder plate. The black glass eyes are a desirable feature.

No. 260 This untypical milliner model has more the look of a wide-eyed child than of a haughty lady. The hair is very plain in front with

No. 259A

No. 259B

No. 260

simple ringlets in back; the neck is short and thick. Although the body is the typical stiff slender type of a milliner model, this one was probably made later during the transition in which the styles were simplified.

Ludwig Greiner, a German immigrant to the United States, and his descendants made dolls from 1858 or earlier to 1900. Papier-mâchés marked with the name "Greiner" are considered desirable for a number of reasons. The Philadelphia, Pennsylvania, origin appeals to American collectors. An 1858 record of the US Letters Patent for reinforcing a doll head with strips of linen makes it possible to document the dolls in a definite period of time. Actually, the Greiners were patterned after dolls that had been made in Europe. Few dolls with characteristics unique to America were developed until the 20th century. Because the Greiner dolls resemble many others of the 19th century, collectors are buying them for their interesting history, not because of their singularity.

A novice should be reminded that a papier-mâché head strengthened with linen is not necessarily a Greiner. The US patent, even with renewal, lasted only 21 years. Any manufacturer could use the idea after the expiration date.

Equally frustrating for the collector, Greiner probably made dolls before securing the patent;—dolls have been found with labels that make no mention of the patent. There are also

No. 262A

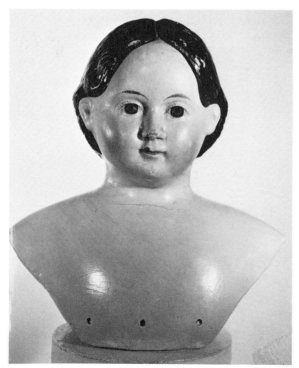

No. 261

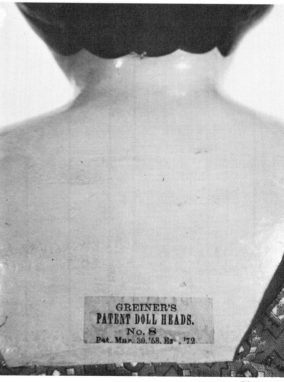

No. 262B

unmarked dolls that may have been made by Greiner and may be older than the marked ones. Although the patent only concerned reinforcing a head, the ingredients for making a doll were listed as paper, Spanish whiting, rye flour, glue and linen.

No. 261 This early Greiner-type has the desirable brown painted eyes and eyelashes. The doll is called a ''Greiner'' type because it does not bear a label, even though labeled examples have been found with the same hair style and manner of decorating. Most of the head is in excellent condition, but there are signs of wear about the nose and mouth, a problem common to many papier-mâchés. The hair is parted in the middle with curls pulled back to show well molded ears. There are three sew holes in the shoulder plate in the fashion of old chinas.

No. 262 A, B This doll has a hair style similar to that found on many common chinas, but it is still an attractive doll because the comb marks have the depth that demonstrate details. There are red lines above the eyes and the upper lids are lined, but there are no eyelashes. The corners of the mouth are turned in a slight smile. As with later chinas, the chest is not as deep and there are no sew holes.

Greiner's Patent label appears on the back.

No. 263 A, B A Greiner with blond hair is not uncommon for a later example with a **72** extension patent label. The nose is sharp, which

No. 263A

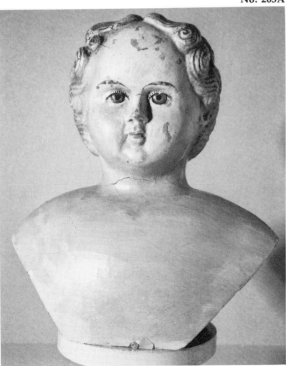

No. 263B

No. 264

gives it a realistic profile, and the hair has complicated swirls of curls; only the lobes of the ear show but they are well formed. The patent label reads:

Greiner's
Patent Doll Heads
No. 13
Pat. March 30 58 Ext. 72

No. 264 This European-made doll illustrates the influence of European tradition on the Greiner dolls. She has the typical painted eyes and blond hair. On the back of her shoulder is the word **Holz-Masse** (papier-mâché) which probably means she was made by the firm Cuno & Otto Dressel who so designated their papier-mâché dolls.

No. 265 A, B Mechanical papier-mâchés often have character faces and perform elaborate actions. The varied actions may include wriggling of fingers, tipping of hats, rocking babies, and playing instruments. The old woman knitting seems to follow her progress with her eyes. She has a wrinkled brow, hair eyelashes, and

cheeks hollowed from age and seems to have a slight smile.

No. 266 Papier-mâché twins with Negroid features, made in the late 19th century, are fairly common. They have glass eyes with no pupils, orange mouths, and wool fiber hair. The white flannel costumes with red cotton collars are made with little attention to details. The cheaply made stiff body is stuffed with excelsior. The arms are papier-mâché, but the orange and black legs have a varnish which could classify them as composition.

No. 267 This 15-inch doll is another example of a papier-mâché from the 1880s (such dolls are commonly found). The doll has multi-stroke eyebrows, glass eyes, and fat cheeks. The original brown wig with bangs and curls is made of mohair. The cloth body is stuffed with excelsior, while the arms and legs are made of composition. The "as found" underwear has an advertisement for Munsingwear.

No. 268 A, B This 10-inch character boy has big blue eyes and a watermelon smile; when he is squeezed, he tips his hat and squeaks. Only

No. 265A

No. 265B

No. 266

No. 268A

No. 267

No. 268B

the head is papier-mâché; his hat is made of corduroy, while his arms and legs are wood with wire attachments. He wears a red and white shirt, dark blue and white pants, and a yellow hat with a red band. This papier-mâché imp strongly resembles the bisque googlies of the 20th century.

Metal

Metal dolls have never been particularly prized and some collectors have childhood memories of lovely broken bisque heads being replaced with the less lifelike metal ones. Certainly such memories would not add to the endearment of metal dolls. Paint on metal frequently peels, also quenching the collector's appetite. Deterioration can be slowed, however, by storing the doll away from extreme temperatures.

No. 269 While dolls made with metal were usually cheaper, in a few instances bisque heads of approximately the same size were less expensive than the metal heads. In 1980 Butler Brothers

No. 270

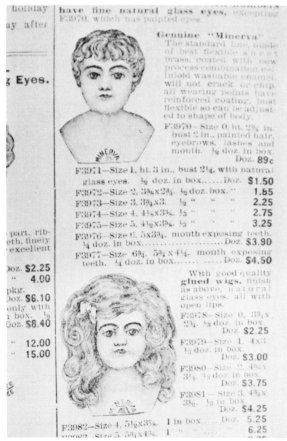

No. 269

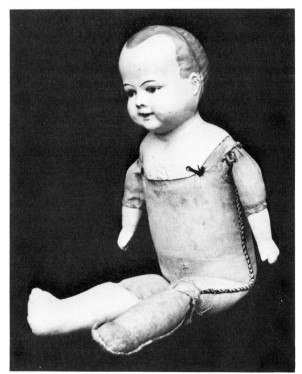

No. 271

catalog advertised a bisque head with side part curly wig and ribbon for $2.25 a dozen. The illustrated metal ones with the German trademark **Minerva** had a side part wig and ribbon and were sold for $4.25 a dozen. Both examples have open mouths and solid glass eyes. Today's collectors are surprised to find that Butler Brothers claimed that "the Minerva doll enjoys a reputation equal to Kestner brand of dolls."

No. 270 The painted eye Minervas with closed mouths were about 30 cents cheaper per dozen than the glass-eyed open mouth examples and were listed at $4.25 per dozen. The not especially well-shaped body is cloth stuffed with hair. The **Minerva** trademark is distinct.

No. 271 A metal baby with a 6-¾ circumference head is marked with the word **Minerva** on the front of the chest. On the back is the numeral **3**. The blue eyes have pupils with white highlights and red lines above the lids. Red dots are found at the corners of the eyes and the nostrils. The one-stroke brown brows match the color of the hair which has comb marks radiating from the crown of the head. The molded ears have excellent details. Stuffed with hair, the original body has chubby bisque hands.

No. 272 One-inch metal frozen Charlottes were given as prizes in Cracker Jacks. The doll is made of an inexpensive metal that fuses at a low temperature. The tiny head has a flat top hairdo and molded eyes, nose, and mouth. This is definitely classified as a doll since there is no loop for it to be used as a charm. There was no attempt to paint the dolls.

No. 273 Jointed charms designed to resemble dolls have fascinated collectors for years. Clara Fawcett described an ancient jointed figure

No. 272

of gold in *Dolls, A New Guide for Collectors*. These four charms are made of a yellow metal decorated with the enameled colors of red, green, purple, and black. No face has the same features. Each was packaged in an envelope with the words **Tony Sarg Marionette Charms**. It is assumed these were made before the death of Sarg in the early 1940s.

No. 273

Wood

Wood is among the oldest material used for dolls. For most of doll history, wood has been an inexpensive material, but in the 20th century wooden dolls have become more and more expensive. The cost of labor appears to have been the main cause. One of the charms of the hand-carved wooden doll is that every doll has its own personality, for there will always be variations even in the same style of doll.

No. 274 The most common wood doll is the so-called Dutch (a corruption of the German word *Deutsch*) wooden. Though Dutch woodens were made in many countries besides Germany, the name appears permanently attached to them. The *Wonderland of Work,* published in the 1880s, stated that one doll company bought 30,000 Dutch dolls every week, and that about 20 dozen dolls could be produced each day. No wonder the doll is common. This crude 7-inch doll, in the style of the Dutch wooden, is jointed by wooden pegs at the shoulders, elbows, hips, and knees. The face is painted with little attention to detail. The eyes are uneven and the mouth is lopsided.

No. 275 A, B This example is also peg-jointed, but the similarity stops there. The doll has a long lady-like neck, a style often found on the milliner models. The slender arms, which are an exaggerated length, have hands simply carved with only an indication for the thumb. The comb in the hair and the painted tendrils of curls which softly frame the face are desirable features, increasing the value of the doll. The doll, which resembles one in the Victoria and Albert Museum, is estimated to have been made sometime between 1825 and 1835.

No. 276 A, B Mason and Taylor, who produced dolls at Springfield, Vt., obtained a patent in 1881 for a swivel-neck doll with a metal rod. The head, made of composition, resembles the china dolls that were fashionable at that time. The eyes, however, have a dark ring around the iris, a style that was frequently used in papier-mâché dolls. Unfortunately for collectors, the peeling paint is not an unusual condition for Mason and Taylor dolls. Pin-jointed limbs of the body must have made the doll a delight to many children, because the dolls could be placed in many positions. This doll is judged a later one because its one original hand is metal instead of

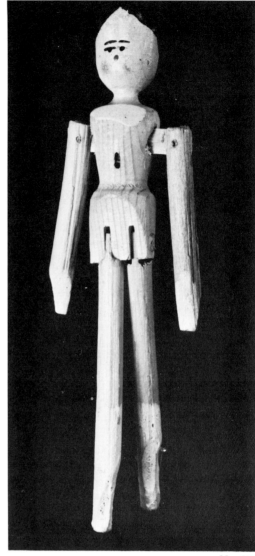

No. 274

the wooden type used earlier. (The other hand is a replacement). The clothes of most Mason and Taylor dolls should be classified "as found" because only the witch and wizard dolls wore factory-made costumes. Although other dolls, such as those by Joel Ellis, were also made in Springfield, there were more Mason and Taylor dolls made than any other type.

No. 277 A Norwegian bride and groom made by Hilda Ege, a Norwegian artist, have the natural grain of wood left untinted on the face with the exception of the eyes, brows, and mouth. The groom is dressed in a blue woolen jacket, black britches, and red vest. The bride has a red wool dress and the linen hand-

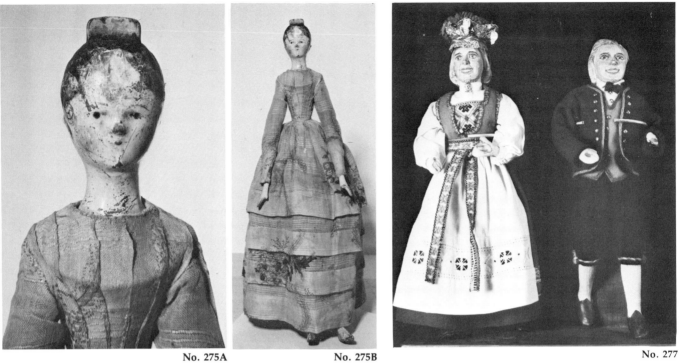

No. 275A   No. 275B   No. 277

embroidered apron which is treasured in Norway as a family heirloom. Hilda Ege dolls became popular in the United States during the 1930s.

Nos. 278, 279 An all-wooden baby face and bent leg baby body, this doll appears to have been inspired by the bisque head German babies. The 8-½-inch circumference head has

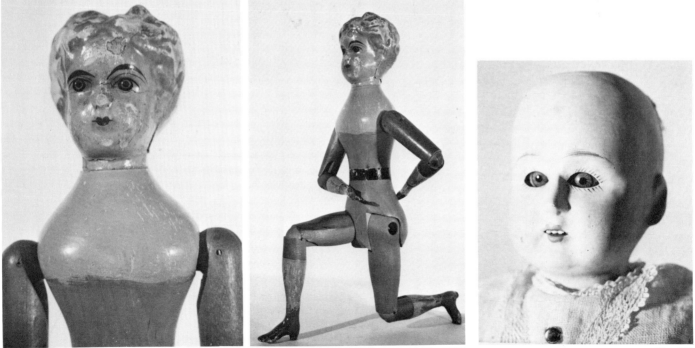

No. 276A   No. 276B   No. 278

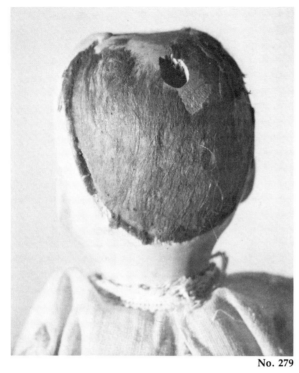

No. 279

No. 280

painted hair and set blue eyes, open mouth with teeth, and a swivel neck. The back of the head, which no longer is covered with the pink complexion coat, shows the texture of the wood.

No. 280 Wooden dolls are still made by commercial companies in England. This one is made of balsam wood and is very light for a wooden doll. The face is almost flat with the exception of its pyramid nose. The large brown eyes are surrounded by thick upper and lower painted black lashes. The cheeks are splashed with light pink without any effort at blending in contrast to the lips which are a bright red. The synthetic carrot red hair goes well with the green cotton print dress. The body is made of cotton. The doll so far has not been sold outside of England.

No. 281 Now that wooden spools are rarely manufactured, these homemade dolls will be found with less frequency. In this one the bottom rim of the spool head has been cut off, and the top of the spool is covered with hair made of wool yarn. The doll has joints, made by metal hooks at the neck, elbows, waist, and knees. The clothes are made of black satin and white faille.

Wax

Because few wax dolls are marked, collectors usually are compelled to judge a wax specimen by its own merit instead of by the reputation of the manufacturer. Dollers interested in collecting dolls of any type of material would be wise to follow this example. Because bisques now outnumber waxes, collectors sometimes forget that the wax dolls were also mass-produced. An 1877 issue of *Harper's Bazaar* stated that some of the English companies produced "thousands of dolls" a week. A collector can't help but wonder what happened to all these English waxes.

The fragility of waxes has been overemphasized in recent years. It is not unusual for a Southern novice to be hesitant about purchasing a wax for fear it will disintegrate in a hot climate. Ironically, a Butler Brothers catalog stated that it would take no responsibility for breakage of wax dolls in shipment during cold weather, not warm. In modern homes there is little to fear from either weather extreme.

When a damaged wax is acquired, the collector faces the problem of whether restoration should be attempted.

In order of availability, the three main categories of waxes are wax-coated, poured-wax and solid-wax. In the 18th century, the English poured-wax dolls usually were the most expensive. That remains true today. Papier-mâché or composition was the most popular base material. When considering a wax doll, a novice should realize that the coating of wax can be so thick that a doll may resemble a poured-wax. Only a poured-wax will be truly translucent. Also, unscrupulous dealers have been known to wax a composition doll for the first time and claim it is a rewaxed doll. Although many consider that rewaxing decreases the value of a doll, a rewaxed example often sells for more than the same type doll that has never had a wax coating. Because all the old wax is removed in the rewaxing process,

No. 282A

No. 281

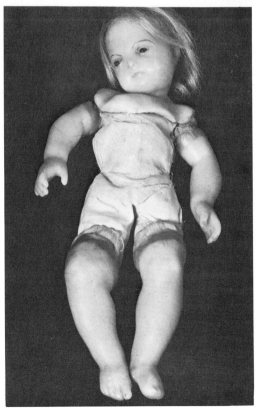

No. 282B

it is almost impossible to judge the doll's original condition.

The color of the rewaxed doll is less mellow than that of old wax. The features sometimes are painted with brighter colors and less skill. In the old factories, workers were assigned assembly line tasks, repeating the same job. The artists acquired by sheer practice a proficiency rarely equalled by modern restorers.

No. 282 A, B This poured wax has the inset blond human hair, put in strand by strand. The strands are placed to imitate the way hair grows on the human head, including the swirl. When held to a light, the mellow yellow wax has a translucent quality. Except for a faint line on the left ankle, there are no signs of age cracks on the wax. The head does almost touch the shoulder, which may mean that the doll has been exposed to extreme heat, perhaps by being placed in an attic. The brown paper weight eyes with tiny black pupils have molded upper and lower lids. The upper lid has a brown line above it, dots at the corner and at the nostrils. Both ears have detailed molding, but the left ear is slightly flatter. Perhaps an object was pressed against the ear, but there is no other sign of flattening.

No. 284

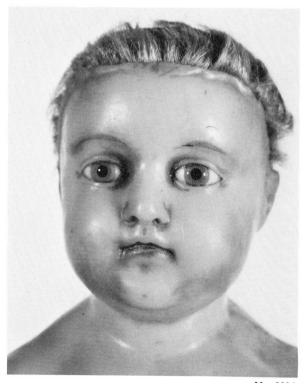

No. 283A

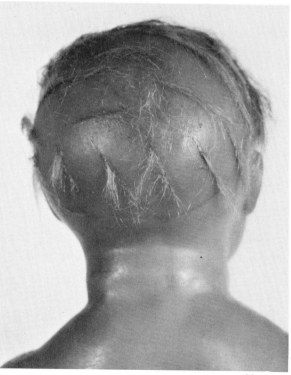

No. 283B

No. 283 A, B Most of the poured waxes have hair inserted on the head by slicing the head with a knife and placing several strands of hair at one time. Unless the head is closely inspected, this method can easily be mistaken for the strand-by-strand process. Because the knife method is more common, the dolls usually are less expensive than other poured-waxes.

No. 284 English in origin, this composition doll with a wax coating has a brown human hair wig which is attached by a deep cut in the head. Collectors call this a "split wig." Numerous cracks radiate from the cut at the top of the forehead almost to the eyebrows. Unfortunately, this is not unusual for this type doll. In fact, if a split-wig doll is discovered without such cracks, it is wise to examine it for the possibility of a rewaxed treatment. This 14-½-inch doll has set glass eyes. The one-stroke brows start at the bridge of the nose. English split-wigs were popular in the early 1880s.

No. 285 A, B Unlike No. 282 which seems to have been a Sunday-best doll, this 24-inch wax doll was intended to be played with by a child. The blue eyes can be opened or closed by a wire on the left side of the body. In the earliest wire-eyed dolls, made around 1825, the wire was placed in the stomach; on more modern specimens, made in the late 19th century, the wire was placed in the back of the head; this is a middle-age example. The very round face has eyebrows which are made with one stroke of the paintbrush but it lacks eyelashes. Two red orange dots indicate the nostrils and a darker orange line separates the lips. The doll has a human hair wig and cloth body with kid arms. The "as found" clothing consists of a cotton chemise.

No. 286 Comic strip characters made of bisque, cloth, and wood are well known to collectors, but German wax examples are often a surprise. With the exception of the stationary heads, Uncle Walt and Skeezix of Gasoline Alley appear almost identical to the all-bisque variety. Uncle Walt has a tiny white cap on top of his yellow molded hair, the shirt is yellow, the bow tie is

No. 285A   No. 285B

No. 286

are made of cloth dipped in a wax material and then draped on her with care to emphasize the natural folds and creases of the clothes. Her flowered red and blue bandana is made the same way. She carries a wax-coated basket filled with six pralines containing a generous amount of "pecans," actually seeds. The Vargas dolls were made of very fragile wax and the fingers are easily damaged. Stamped on the bottom of her wooden base are the words **Genuine Vargas, New Orleans, La.** The word "Genuine" may indicate that the Vargas dolls were copied.

No. 288 This character has the protruding eyes but with smaller pupils, prominent cheek

red and the pants are blue, and the shoes are gray. Made of wax with a dull yellow color, he has black brows, black eyes, and if his mouth was ever decorated the paint has since flaked away. He is 3-½ inches tall. Skeezix is 2-⅝ inches tall and made of the same type wax. His hair is pale yellow, the shirt is white with a floppy red tie, the pants are green, and he has white socks and brown shoes. These dolls were made strictly for export because before World War II the average German had no knowledge of our "funny papers."

No. 287 The wax figures made by the Vargas family of New Orleans, though not designed to be playthings, often win in competition with real dolls. The founder of the Vargas dynasty immigrated from Mexico in the middle of the 18th century. His specialty was religious figures. Doll collectors are more familar with the work of his granddaughter, Lucy Rosado, who created a variety of some sixty character figures. She never made more than seven or eight a day. In the 1950s she discontinued her creations.

The Praline Vender is typical of the Vargas street people of New Orleans. She has the protruding black eyes, molded eyebrows, broad flattened nose, full lips, and kinky wax hair. Her green polka dotted dress, red kerchief and apron

No. 287

No. 288

No. 289A

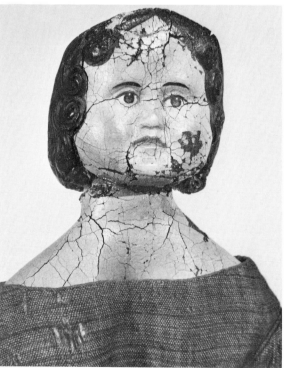

No. 289B

bones and an open-closed mouth. He wears a battered straw hat and red bandana tied at the neck, a printed shirt and gray trousers that give the appearance of great wear. In his left hand he holds a bunch of bananas. Found on his base is the paper label **Harriet's, 318 Royal Street, New Orleans, La.,** and the stamped words **Vargas, New Orleans.** Like the Praline Vender, he is 6 inches tall, excluding the base.

Old Rubber

Twentieth century rubber dolls still turn up

in second-hand stores, but older rubber specimens come to light only occasionally. Most of them are the hard, painted shoulder-head type. Often they are chipped or even broken, many are almost without paint. A novice usually ignores these dolls because of the condition and almost-destroyed beauty, but many seasoned collectors cherish these hard luck specimens.

The less common soft or vulcanized type are too often left flat on their backs in attics. Because of this they often are found melted out of shape by years of high summer temperatures or badly cracked from long cold winters.

No. 289 A, B Some collectors credit the Goodyear Co. with the first doll patent because the ingredients of their formulas were patented in 1853. This rubber doll is typical of a middle 19th century rubber doll. Here again is a material imitating a hairstyle popular with china dolls. The hair is a flat-top style, parted in the middle with tight curls at the temples and cheeks. The back of the hair, which shows less deterioration, has excellent comb marks. The face has fewer contours than a china of the era. The mouth is solemn and unsmiling. The brows are painted with one heavy stroke, and the dark eyes have a tiny, white highlight.

No. 290 A, B This soft rubber 8 ¾-inch boy never had any paint except the white of the eyes and the red on the lips, which is almost mint. The uniform blackness of the body would indicate that the rubber was colored before molding. The coloring material probably was carbon, or "lamp black," used in many black rubber products. Although there is some graining of surface texture, the doll is soft to the touch and still en-

No. 290B

No. 290A

tirely flexible. The doll is pitch black, but is not a Negro. The torso has wide sloping shoulders and the gourd-shaped abdomen of the very old bisques, both French and German. The arms and legs are molded with all the ridges of fat that were the signs of a healthy happy baby in the 1800s. All the limbs are easily moved in a full circle and still hold many positons.

One of the most interesting features of this doll is the manner in which the arms and legs are attached. The joints seem to be similar to those used in modern plastic dolls. Sturdy, pointed thorns must have been molded on the flat upper ends of the limbs, and holes, or soft spots, centered in the flat hip and shoulder flanges. Once these thorns were thrust through the holes, the arrowheads kept them pulled out but permitted the full-circle movement on the thorn shaft.

The joints of this rubber doll seems to fit the French patent of 1858 granted to Thomas Hammond. The patient was for invisible joints on vulcanized rubber dolls. Because it could hardly be considered a French doll, the suspicion arises that some German manufacturer made use of this patent with or without permission.

Modern Rubber

No. 291 Distinguished doll designers such as Rose O'Neill and Grace Storey Putnam have created interesting examples in this material. But of all the rubber dolls produced in the twentieth century, none seem to enjoy more popularity with collectors than the Hummel dolls. These

No. 291

dolls were inspired by the drawings of a German nun, Sister Maria Innocentia and manufactured by the Goebel factory. Unfortunately the Hummel creations can withstand heat, but storage in a damp place has a disastrous effect.

They were later reissued in a more durable plastic material.

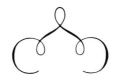

Plastics

There are those who argue that since plastics are mass-produced and unbreakable, these dolls do not deserve to be called collectible. Yet there has never been a medium in which dolls were made that has not become collectible. Even dolls made of soap have been displayed at the Smithsonian Institution.

Another point to ponder is that vinyl dolls now face a critical stage of development. Throughout our century the change in materials for dollmaking has reflected the major historical upheavals. World War I gave the American composition manufacturers a chance to dominate the doll market temporarily. The inflation and depression in Europe helped destroy the bisque manufacturers, including Armand Marseille and Kestner. World War II forced American companies to try new materials, plastic and vinyl.

Today, collectors are wondering if increased cost and petroleum shortages will affect the production of plastic dolls. Some conservationists have advised Americans to avoid buying dolls and toys made of plastic since petroleum, an important ingredient in their production is more needed elsewhere. If this sentiment becomes a strong force, then certainly a change looms ahead for the doll world. Increased petroleum costs lead inevitably to higher prices for plastic. These dolls may not only become more expensive, but less plentiful.

Skeptics may demand stronger evidence of desirability. Advertisements for plastic dolls, both wanted and for sale, frequently appear in magazines usually specializing in antiques, such as *Spinning Wheel.* For another gauge of collector interest, in 1974, Madame Alexander, founder of one of the most respected of American doll companies, was enthusiastically received as a guest speaker at a national doll convention whose membership normally collects only antique dolls.

So far there is no simple criteria for judging the quality of plastic other than the brand name and subject of the doll. Unlike the bisque dolls, an open or closed mouth on a plastic doll matters little. The hair style, so important in Parian and china, is often changed by a child. The hard plastics are sometimes considered better because they were made earlier. However both hard and plastic and soft vinyl dolls are currently on the market.

Since plastic dolls comprise the major part of current doll markets, it is hard to remember that there have been dolls of this material for more than three decades.

When Ideal produced the first all-plastic doll in 1939, the event was regarded so revolutionary that the *New York Times* reported it as news.

No. 292 "Marianne Fashion Designing Set," by Laxture Products, Inc., is one of the earliest plastic dolls. Since plastics had yet to be proved as best sellers, she is designed to resemble a composition doll. She is especially interesting because of a printed page that is enclosed in the box.

"To All Young Would Be Stylists. This is a mannequin, not an ordinary doll. She is a miniature of a teenage girl made of a plastic material but not flexible. Because the War Production Program requires rubber which we previously used in manufacture of these mannequins, we are now using a new material to continue making them so that you can do your bit by learning to sew and save."

The leaflet also promises the doll will be durable. In spite of this claim the doll legs are crazed, a

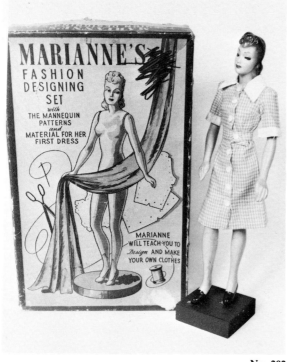

No. 292

common problem that was also true of composition dolls in this era.

The doll came with material for her first dress and a pattern. The leaflet also lists four extra sets of patterns. Each set, which sold for 19¢, consists of three patterns. The mannequin has molded hair and painted features; its jointed arms were assembled by the buyer. Also included was a wooden stand.

No. 293 In the early 1950s, a vinyl example of the Bye-Lo sold for approximately $1 in stores throughout the nation. Today the doll has substantially increased in value. The doll is closer to the creator's (Grace Storey Putnam) original concept of a three-day-old baby than the bisque examples because the rolls of baby fat are more evident. This 15-inch example has painted blue eyes and upper eyelashes. On the back of the head is **(C) Grace Storey Putnam** in big incised letters. The voice box in the cloth body still works. The arms and legs are of plastic.

No. 294 Horsman Doll Company sold a baby doll with the trademark **Bye-Lo**, but it was designed by another artist. Incised on the head is the date **1972,** but the doll was offered for several years. It will be interesting to learn if a doll with only the Bye-Lo name will be as popular with collectors in the future. A nice touch is a pam-

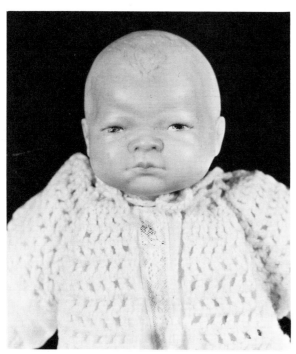

No. 293

No. 294

phlet, included in the box, covering the history of the Horsman dolls.

No. 295 Another famous doll, Shirley Temple, has been reissued several times in vinyl. As with the Bye-Lo, the first time was in the 1950s when Shirley Temple movies were experiencing a revival. The second time was in the 1970s. It was not unusual for a television commercial accompanying an old Shirley Temple movie to promote the new Shirley doll. The Ideal Company marked the new version with the initials **S.T.** instead of the full name.

No. 296 The box is one of the most appealing features of one of the Shirleys sold in the 1970s. It is covered with pictures of Shirley as a little girl. Although a reissue, the face is a new design which bears a closer resemblance to the little actress. No collector is likely to confuse the two issues. The stationary eyes are more like the color of the eyes of real Shirley Temple. Unlike the doll of the 1950s which had many outfits, the current doll is offered for sale with few separate costume

No. 296

No. 295

No. 297

No. 298

No. 299

choices. An unexpected attraction to owning a Shirley Temple Doll was added when, in 1974, Shirley Temple Black was appointed ambassador to Ghana and later became Chief of Protocal for President Ford. It is indeed a novelty to have a doll that represents the child version of a United States ambassador.

The medium of plastic seems well suited for dolls designed for special purposes.

No. 297 In 1950, the "Toni" doll by Ideal was one of the most popular dolls ever made by any company. Each came with a Toni home permanent kit. The doll had a nylon wig that could be washed and set.

No. 298 "Harriet Hubbard Ayer", also made by Ideal, was sold with an elaborate make-up kit. It included lipstick, rouge, powder, eyeshadow, and eyebrow pencil, attached to a cardboard dressing table.

No. 299 Little 8-inch dolls with a big selection of separate wardrobes were popular in the 1950s. "Ginny", first made by the Vogue Company in composition in the 1940s, became the most successful of the 8-inch plastic dolls. By 1954, Ginny could walk and had an amazing 52 separate outfits of clothing. The variety ranged from Dutch costumes, ski outfits complete with skis, and party dresses. Her accessories included a stuffed dog, shoe bag filled with shoes, and four pairs of eyeglasses. This Ginny has her own pink trunk decorated with her name and face. Other companies introduced 8-inch dolls in competition. Each had a different look, but little girls often used their clothes interchangeably. Ginny was reissued in the 1970s. The more recent issue, made in Hong Kong, was still available in department stores in 1975, and sold with three outfits.

No. 300 "Betsy McCall" was inspired by the ever popular paper doll series in *McCall's* magazine. When the doll first appeared on the market it was so successful that many stores found it difficult to keep it in stock. The doll has been made in various sizes from 8 to 36 inches. Also, it has been produced by different companies, such as Ideal and American Character. The 8-inch example by the now dissolved American Character was sold with a separate wardrobe in 1957. Unlike the other 8-inch dolls with wardrobes, Betsy had a less chubby shape.

No. 301 The Kewpies made of vinyl would

No. 300

probably have pleased their creator, Rose O'Neill, very much. In November, 1929 in *Playthings*, Mrs. O'Neill was quoted as saying:

"They (Kewpies) went all 'round the earth made in hard materials, bisque, celluloid, rubber, composition. But I was not satisfied. I wanted a Kewpie that would be soft to the touch, a Kewpie that would melt in your arms."

She further explained that she tried to give the Kewpies "a look that meant "Understanding, Funniness, and Love. And the dolls had to be soft to the touch to express these things. The Kewpie philosophy is soft."

Many vinyl versions have been produced. Some, like "The Thinker," wear no clothes. Others are costumed in dresses, two-piece pajamas, and one-piece nightwear with covered feet. Cameo, Horsman, Strombecker, and Amsco, a division of Milton Bradley, have been granted the right to make dolls with the copyrighted name of Kewpie. As of 1977 the pro-

No. 301

No. 302

No. 303

duction of Kewpies was halted at least temporarily.

No. 302 Cameo made both a composition and later a vinyl version of Scootles, another one of Rose O'Neill's creations.

No. 303 Just as the composition dolls of Alexander have special appeal to collectors, the Alexander plastics are becoming more and more appreciated. For years, all Alexander dolls have been made in America.

The hard plastic "Cissettes" made by Alexander in the late 1950s had elaborate wardrobes. Some of the costumes, such as the coronation dress in imitation of Queen Elizabeth II, cost $9. The clothes were made of expensive materials such as taffeta, brocade, and organdy. Accessories included hats of real straw, hose, and taffeta pants trimmed with lace.

No. 304 In the 1960s, Madame Alexander used the Cissettes mold for the "Portrette Series" of dolls. None in this group was sold with separate clothing. If Cissettes and Portrettes are found undressed, identification difficulty may arise. However, the newer dolls' features are decorated with brighter coloring. They also have eye shadow and painted fingernails.

No. 305 The "Sound of Music" dolls, based on the popular 20th Century Fox movie, are

one of the most popular groups of vinyl dolls. There are two issues also of this group. The larger size was issued in 1964. The smaller size, issued in 1968, was discontinued in 1974. Since the 1964 size is the original, it probably will in-

No. 304

No. 305

crease in value faster than the later ones. Maria bears a strong resemblance to Julie Andrews. The children are dressed in Austrian style clothing. In some cases the same face is used with a different hair style for each character. Madame Alexander uses the same face with different costumes and hair styles in many of her dolls.

No. 306 The dolls of the "International Series, or Friends from Foreign Lands," by Madame Alexander, are generally thought to have the same face, with appearance changes caused by different costumes, wigs, and decorating styles. Actually, there are two different faces in this series. These dolls have been available since the early 1950s. More than twenty years later many stores are still carrying this long-lasting series. The dolls, which are marked **Alex** on the back, are accompanied by a booklet picturing Alexander dolls. Most have a cloth label sewed on clothes, listing the name of the country and the words **By Madame Alexander, New York, U.S.A.**

A blue-eyed blonde of Hungary and a dark-skinned girl of India of the International Series (pictured) share the common face that is recognized by most collectors. Costuming and accessories succeed in making the dolls appear different. The girl of the Far East wears coin earrings,

snake bracelet, a chain necklace, and golden sandals. The Hungarian wears a gold headdress with red and green stones and boots on her feet. Originally the dolls in this series had unbending legs. The ones with jointed knees were made from approximately 1956 to 1972.

No. 307 A Vietnamese peasant girl and a Korean have the more unusual face that is often

No. 306

No. 307

ited States. The chosen six were Martha Washington **(A)**, Abigail Adams **(B)**, Dolly Madison **(C)**, Martha Randolph, Elizabeth Monroe, and Louisa Adams **(D)**. The series continued to be available in 1977.

Richard Toy Company, whose products are manufactured in Hong Kong, made Bicentennial Dolls packaged in a red, white, and blue box. Included in the series are "Gibson Girl," "Flapper" and "New Look 1947." A collector could have an interesting collection of dolls produced in honor of our country's 200th birthday.

No. 310 American companies don't have a monopoly on interesting vinyl dolls inspired by books. A delightful example from England, *Fiona of Thistledown,* is based on Norman Thelwell's humorous books on the tribulations of ponies and riders. "Fiona" is wearing proper riding clothes, but her legs don't quite reach the metal stirrups of the removable saddle. The fat pony has a mane and tail made of real hair and decorated with red ribbons. Other details include a brand on the flank of the pony. The box, one of the most imaginative ever designed for a doll, doubles as a horse trailer. It is decorated with

overlooked. Instead of a rosebud-shaped mouth, both have thin lips that are curved in a gentle smile. The dolls lack dimples and have chins that are flat in appearance when compared to the more typical features of the series. The lesser known face seems to be reserved for a few of the Orientals. It is a reasonable speculation that as more collectors recognize that this exotic face is less used, its value will increase faster than others in the series.

No. 308 Dolls based on characters from books have long been favorites. "Madame Doll" was inspired by *The Secret of Madame Doll,* a children's book about the American revolution. As in the book, the doll has a secret pocket in her petticoat to hide her pearls. This doll, introduced in 1967, could still be purchased in some department stores in 1975. Madame Doll has the same face as other Alexander creations such as Cinderella and Scarlett O'Hara. The elaborate colonial style dress of pink brocade makes her especially interesting.

No. 309 (ABCD) In 1976, Madame Alexander introduced a collection of six presidents' wives in honor of the Bicentennial celebration of the Un-

No. 308

No. 309A

No. 309B

No. 309C

No. 309D

No. 310

No. 311

No. 312

two of Thelwell's famous cartoons. The doll is made by Plasteck International Designs Limited. In the United States these dolls were available for several years through equestrian supply stores.

No. 311 Many of the plastic dolls from Italy are of superior quality. "Bonomi," a hard plastic available in the early 1960s, is considered a collector's item. Among her attractive features are flirting eyes, human hair wig, and excellent kid boots.

No. 312 The "Furga" dolls of Italy range from inexpensive to so expensive that most parents would be reluctant to buy the doll as a plaything. Some of the lady dolls sold for $59.95 in 1975. In contrast, is this little Hawaiian baby, purchased for $3.99 that same year. Regardless of price, **Pablo** dressed in a grass skirt and flowers, has charm. The 6-inch baby came packaged in a transparent pineapple decorated with a felt top. Some of the other small dolls were sold in containers in the shape of pears, apples, and hearts.

No. 313 A 5-inch baby designed by Alma Dejournette during the 1950s came with a com-

plete paper layette and birth certificate. On the front side the blue-eyed baby has great detail, including lifelines in the chubby palms and wrinkles at the knees. The doll is flat and undecorated on the other side. This was an economically clever touch. "My Baby Life Time Plastic Doll" is unusual for another reason. Instead of being produced in New York or a foreign country, it was made in Atlanta, Georgia.

No. 314 At present Barbie is the world's best selling doll. According to Johana Gast Anderton, author of *Twentieth Century Dolls* and *More Twentieth Century Dolls,* by 1974 more than 80 million Barbies had been sold. Many collectors doubt that such a common doll deserves a place in a collection. Certainly the most popular doll has historical appeal, even if it has little monetary value. Barbie cost $3 when she was introduced by Mattel in 1958. Many of the costumes which were sold separately were more expensive than the doll, ranging from $1 to $5. The entire wardrobe of 19 sets, which retailed at $51.10, included Barbie Q outfit, Easter Parade, Peachy-Fleechy coat, and Wedding Day clothes. Some of

No. 313

No. 314

No. 315

the costumes which represented the ultimate in high fashion seem quite amusing now. This original Barbie is wearing a "Gay Parisienne Costume," which was described as "Top fashion news of Paris." The balloon-shaped skirt was a short-lived style. The outfit cost $4.

At first there were brunette and blond Barbies; but for the past few years all Barbies have been blond. Perhaps the brunette some day will be the most valuable. Many mistakenly refer to Barbie as the first doll with an adult figure, but the Armand Marseille lady doll illustrated in the German chapter was made more than 30 years before Barbie was created.

No. 315 The manufacturers of plastic dolls have been ingenious in creating new markets.

Many boys now play with articulated figures of soldiers and cowboys, which are really dolls. Usually these are made in a series and have extra equipment such as horses, pup tents and different clothes. Villains as well as heroes are often included in a series.

The Mego Corporation, whose products are made in Hong Kong, markets heroes of the comics, such as Batman and Superman. One of the most unusual is the "Planet of the Apes" group, based on the science fiction book and 20th Century Fox movies. During 1974, while the television program of that name was enjoying a brief life, the 8-inch action figures were highly advertised. In 1975, there were five figures in the series, four apes and one astronaut. Accessories included an ape's treehouse, a village, and a horse. The whole group is cleverly listed on the back of a 1975 package in hopes that the purchaser will be tempted to obtain a complete set.

Other companies also produced ape figures, a good indication of the success of the doll. Children might discern little difference in the figures but collectors would prefer the authorized versions. Some collectors may find them ugly, but since the faces of the apes cannot be used as other characters their singularity may make them

Campbell Kids, and Pillsbury Dough Boy are examples.

No. 316 The "Sun Maid" doll in 1974 was available in department stores. However, a child's dress had to be purchased before obtaining the 23-inch doll. She is larger and more expensive than most advertising dolls. Made of soft vinyl, she has brown sleeping eyes and black ringlet curls. The long dress and matching bonnet are covered with pictures of boxes of raisins. The price of the dress and unavailability in certain areas may be factors in classifying her as one of the rarest advertising dolls produced in the mid-1970s.

No. 317 A new era began in the history of vinyl dolls when the manufacturers recognized the possibility that vinyl dolls appeal to adults as well as to children. Some dolls are more likely to be purchased for collections than for playthings.

In 1974 this 12-inch Indian boy and girl were ordered from the Jack Wolf Catalog, Salt Lake City, Utah. Both are dressed in purple suede and have the same smiling face with inset marble-like eyes. The boy carries a bow and has a quiver of arrows strapped to his back; a rabbit, tied to his other hand, represents his game. The girl

No. 316

attractive to collectors. Mego also made a small size ape which was cheaper.

Advertising dolls are considered extremely collectible. Such dolls are usually made for a limited period. Often the design can be used for only one particular doll. The unavailability of offers in some areas limits the numbers of collectors who can acquire the dolls. There is so much interest that a group of collectors have established an exchange program where premiums for a doll offered in one area only can be swapped for those available in another.

A few advertising dolls are sold without premiums being necessary. Charlie the Tuna,

No. 317

No. 318

holds a leather fish and has a papoose strapped to her back. Both labels are identified:

"Carlson Doll, a collector's item, not an ordinary toy. Manufactured with the founders of America in mind to keep Americans aware of our heritage. Made in U.S.A."

Their heart-shaped stands have the name **Carlson** imprinted on the bottom.

No. 318 In August 1974, Effanbee Doll Company became a pioneer in the making of numbered limited edition dolls with the founding of the Effanbee Limited Edition Doll Club. Through mail and periodical advertisements the company offered anyone the opportunity to purchase "Precious Baby." Orders were filled until 2,880 dolls were ordered, or until January 31, 1975,

when the molds for the doll were destroyed, never to be created again. Each doll was accompanied by a certificate listing the number of the doll in order of production and name of purchaser. Special labels sewn inside the dress and on the body also state that the doll is a limited edition. The original price of this premiere doll was $40; no one can guess accurately what the price will be in years to come. In 1977, a self portrait of Dewees Cochran, distinguished American doll artist, was offered. If this new venture is well received, perhaps there will be a limited edition Barbie, Scarlett O'Hara, and Betsy McCall. Regardless of possible competition in the future, Effanbee can always claim with justifiable pride that Precious Baby was the first.

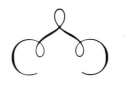

The Art of Winning Ribbons

Winning ribbons in a Doll Show of any kind is a calculated art. It combines knowledge, instinct, and imagination in displaying dolls at their best. How much a doll costs is less important. Too often the example with the best chance of winning is left at home and overlooked because it was a bargain or a less publicized doll.

No. 319 Of course, some collectors will have dolls worthy of competition in the most expensive categories. This 25-inch French Schmitt, with a fashion type kid body, won Best-in-Show at a regional convention in 1975. She is all original, including her Spanish costume complete with mantilla. It is interesting to note that several fine Brus were in competition.

Here are a few basic points that may increase chances of garnering a ribbon in less expensive types.

First, it is important to know your doll, especially the origin and period of manufacture. If either estimate is inaccurate, the doll will probably be disqualified. Waiting to consult with an expert at the show or convention is little help; most shows have rules that a doll, once entered, cannot be switched to another category. Do your research before show time.

Too many entrants fail to fill out entries exactly as asked. One collector entered a category called "Wardrobe made by collector." The requirements asked that each outfit be described. Instead, the collector reported that she was duplicating the dresses shown and described for Lettie Lane's doll as illustrated in an old *Ladies Home Journal*. The entry was disqualified because each piece was not separately described as asked.

If you are unsure about a requirement for entering or displaying dolls, write and ask the exhibit chairman. Although it was not specified to mount clothes, at one convention this was a requirement. A Bru with an original wardrobe was disqualified because the clothes were displayed loosely on the table.

Dollhouse dolls are usually required to be shown tied together or on stands.

Doll Shows sponsored by clubs usually have knowledgeable judges. The categories often vary

No. 319

from year to year. However, the dolls earn ribbons based on quality and condition.

No. 320 A, B, C A magnificent example of a glass-eyed Parian won first prize at the Leticia Penn 22nd Anniversary May 14, 1969.

Fairs

Few dolls can win ribbons every place they are entered. A long face Jumeau might win a blue ribbon at a Doll Show and not even place at a Fair. In many instances the judges at the Fairs have little knowledge and pick the winners by costume rather than quality. Many collectors decide that it is not worth risking damage to fragile dolls if the judges have had meager exposure to dolls. For Fair competition, entering novelty examples might be better than submitting antique specimens.

One of the authors dressed a wooden peg doll in a peddler outfit and filled her pockets with little Frozen Charlotte dolls. She won in the "most unusual" category at a Fair; at a Doll Show she would have been disqualified since she was not an authentic peddler. Dolls made of material such as sponge, rocks, and peanuts often make good impressions on non-collectors.

Flashy foreign dressed dolls have a better chance in Fairs than the more unusual understated dolls such as a Kathe Kruse. Foreign men have less entries than foreign women.

Keep in mind insurance companies often exclude dolls from coverage if entered in Fairs. In contrast, most national doll conventions insure each doll while exhibited.

Regional Shows

A prize winner at a national show is not necessarily a winner at a regional one. A rare French A.T. failed to receive any prize at a regional convention. At some of the regional conventions, all collectors have a vote. The owner forgot that few have an opportunity to examine an A.T. She neglected to include a card with the doll's mark. Unrecognized, it was passed over for a more common French example.

It is not true that winning in a regional convention is a popularity contest. Such conventions usually have between 200 and 400 people attending. The average club does not have enough members to become much of a voting block. A doll so rare that it is not known to the majority of collectors will have little chance.

Because members are not allowed to

No. 320A

No. 320B

No. 320C

No. 321

No. 322

examine dolls, it is a good idea to include a typed card describing the doll and its mark. List the outstanding features as well. A doll with a replaced part or a minor repair has a better chance at a regional convention with mass voting than at a National. At a regional, dolls can win without all original clothing, it helps if it is dressed in old materials and in an authentic style.

The art of displaying a doll makes a difference. At one convention, practically all babies were dressed in freshly pressed white dresses. The prize winning "Laughing Baby", a Gerbruder Heubach, **No. 102**, illustrated in "Babies" wore a slightly faded pink dress and held a much worn and loved stuffed dog. Included in competition were a **J.D.K.** "Hilda" and a rare Davies & Voetch.

No. 321 Baby with original moleskin wig, incised **J.D.K.** won second prize. The impression the doll makes is more important than the mark.

No. 322 The A.M. doll (also pictured in **No. 58** in German Dolls) has won over older and more

expensive dolls such as the Kestner Gibson girls. Perhaps the flapper clothes conjure up fond memories. So far she has garnered five ribbons.

No. 323 A smiling Fashion with original clothing is a striking doll. She is a regional blue ribbon winner.

Dolls which duplicate the theme of a regional convention have an added appeal. It is obvious that a Gibson girl would attract more attention if Charles Dana Gibson creations are the symbols of the convention. A bonnet doll resembling Kate Greenaway drawings would be a good candidate at a show honoring the artist. "Gone With the Wind" paper dolls won first prize at Atlanta.

National Shows and Conventions

At such shows the dolls are sometimes undressed and usually the examples are examined from head to toes. Replaced arms or legs can cost points, but you should leave a damaged part instead of substituting a reproduction.

No. 324 Damaged dolls can win ribbons. Although this unusual bonnet has a crack on her head, the exquisite details on the bonnet helped her earn a third prize at a National Convention in 1973. In 1974, she won the blue ribbon. Old clothing, even if tattered, should not be removed. The tears might even add to the charm of a doll. An example needs to have some unusual characteristics as well as old clothing.

No. 325 This all original Parian is worthy of ribbons. She has blond molded hair, glass eyes, and a Civil War mourning costume. She won a second place at a National Convention in 1973.

No. 326 Charlie Chaplin with his original tramp-like clothing earned third place in "celebrity" category. A doll representing John Bundy won first place that year.

Some collectors buy dolls for the old clothing and transfer the costume to a more unusual doll. In fairness to other collectors, label such clothes

No. 324

No. 323

No. 325

No. 326

have a definite theme and be as all original as possible.

No. 327 The wedding party prize winner at two conventions is dressed in all original crepe paper costumes, including flower covered hats. Separately and undressed, these all bisques would not be remarkable but as a unit they are attention getters. These dolls have been retired from competition because they have won a blue ribbon at a National Convention.

Typed cards describing your dolls are also recommended at a National Convention. This insures the judges will not overlook the doll's special qualities.

Regional and National

It is a mistake to assume that an expensive doll will be the best bet to win. Perhaps to justify the money spent, many collectors enter the traditionally expensive categories, such as French Children and Parians. Remember, usually only four or five ribbons are awarded, depending whether or not honorable mention is included. The more offbeat categories such as Fortune Tellers, American Mechanical, and Religious Dolls have less entries.

No. 328 A representation of Baby Jesus, 10 inches tall, won second place at a National Convention. He has a wax head and arms, and a stuffed body. The blond wig is original.

as old, *not* original. When a category is offered for groups, the competition is always stiff. To have a chance on winning, the group should

No. 327

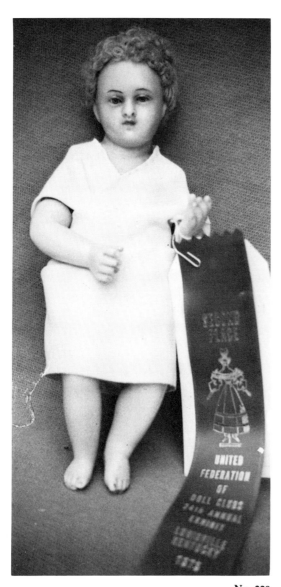

No. 328

No. 329A

No. 329 A, B This two-face Kewpie-Billikin celluloid is a good example of an inexpensive doll that can win. He was bought through a mail order ad for $15. in 1973. He won a white ribbon at a regional convention over several more expensive examples. He was just so different. Also, he was displayed with a mirror so both faces could be seen.

No. 330 In contrast, a third place winner is an example of the expensive dolls that are found

No. 329B

No. 330

No. 331

in the category of French Child. Unmarked, she has lamb's wool wig, closed mouth, original underwear, and shoes.

No. 331 This Bru with a wooden body is another example of the exquisite dolls that are found in French categories. She is a blue ribbon winner from a regional, but has yet to win a national.

Dollhouse Dolls of Other Material than China or Bisque is another category in which there are fewer entries. Also few collectors par-

ticipate in the 30-inch or over categories; it takes more effort to bring such large dolls, and also, fewer collectors have the space to own such large dolls.

One of the dangers of buying a doll in an offbeat category is that the category may be discontinued. Even such a popular category as "German Babies" has occasionally been eliminated due to lack of space. But divisions have a way of resurfacing another time.

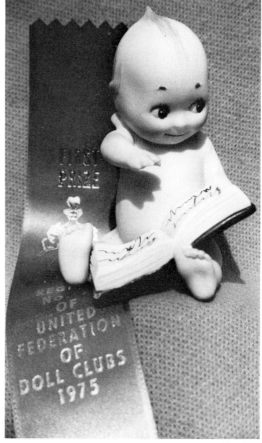

No. 332

No. 333

No. 332 Action Kewpies are the best bets to win in the bisque Kewpie category. The Kewpie with the cat has won at both national and regional conventions.

No. 333 The Kewpie with the book won a blue ribbon at a regional convention, has never been entered in national competition.

Don't give up on a doll because it doesn't win at a convention, especially if it is something special. One collector gave a Kestner Googlie one last chance to win a ribbon. It had been shown at two conventions without success. At the third convention it captured the blue ribbon!

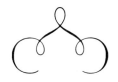

Index